❖ ANCIENT WORLD LEADERS ❖

HAMMURABI

◆ ◆ ◆

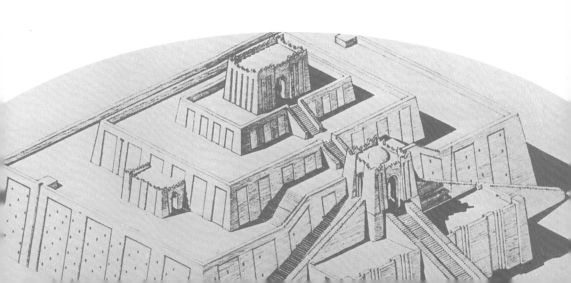

❖ ANCIENT WORLD LEADERS ❖

HAMMURABI

JUDITH LEVIN

CHELSEA HOUSE
PUBLISHERS
An imprint of Infobase Publishing

Frontispiece: Head of a king, possibly Hammurabi. From Susa. Housed in the Louvre, Paris, France.

Hammurabi
Copyright © 2009 by Infobase Publishing

All rights reserved. No part of this book may be reproduced or utilized in any form or by any means, electronic or mechanical, including photocopying, recording, or by any information storage or retrieval systems, without permission in writing from the publisher. For information, contact:

Chelsea House
An imprint of Infobase Publishing
132 West 31st Street
New York, NY 10001

Library of Congress Cataloging-in-Publication Data

Levin, Judith (Judith N.), 1956–
  Hammurabi / Judith Levin.
    p. cm. — (Ancient world leaders)
  Includes bibliographical references and index.
  ISBN 978-0-7910-9603-1 (hardcover)
  1. Hammurabi, King of Babylonia. 2. Babylonia—History. 3. Babylonia—Kings and rulers—Biography. I. Title. II. Series.
  DS73.35.L48 2008
  935'.02—dc22   2008004866
  [B]

Chelsea House books are available at special discounts when purchased in bulk quantities for businesses, associations, institutions, or sales promotions. Please call our Special Sales Department in New York at (212) 967-8800 or (800) 322-8755.

You can find Chelsea House on the World Wide Web at http://www.chelseahouse.com

Text design by Lina Farinella
Cover design by Jooyoung An

Printed in the United States of America

Bang NMSG 10 9 8 7 6 5 4 3 2 1

This book is printed on acid-free paper.

All links and Web addresses were checked and verified to be correct at the time of publication. Because of the dynamic nature of the Web, some addresses and links may have changed since publication and may no longer be valid.

❖ CONTENTS ❖

Arthur M. Schlesinger, Jr.
On Leadership

Leadership, it may be said, is really what makes the world go round. Love no doubt smoothes the passage; but love is a private transaction between consenting adults. Leadership is a public transaction with history. The idea of leadership affirms the capacity of individuals to move, inspire, and mobilize masses of people so that they act together in pursuit of an end. Sometimes leadership serves good purposes, sometimes bad; but whether the end is benign or evil, great leaders are those men and women who leave their personal stamp on history.

Now, the very concept of leadership implies the proposition that individuals can make a difference. This proposition has never been universally accepted. From classical times to the present day, eminent thinkers have regarded individuals as no more than the agents and pawns of larger forces, whether the gods and goddesses of the ancient world or, in the modern era, race, class, nation, the dialectic, the will of the people, the spirit of the times, history itself. Against such forces, the individual dwindles into insignificance.

So contends the thesis of historical determinism. Tolstoy's great novel *War and Peace* offers a famous statement of the case. Why, Tolstoy asked, did millions of men in the Napoleonic Wars, denying their human feelings and their common sense, move back and forth across Europe slaughtering their fellows? "The war," Tolstoy answered, "was bound to happen simply because it was bound to happen." All prior history determined it. As for leaders, they, Tolstoy said, "are but the labels that serve to give a name to an end and, like labels, they have the least possible connection with the event." The greater the leader, "the more conspicuous the inevitability and the predestination of every act he commits." The leader, said Tolstoy, is "the slave of history."

Determinism takes many forms. Marxism is the determinism of class. Nazism the determinism of race. But the idea of men and women as the slaves of history runs athwart the deepest human instincts. Rigid determinism abolishes the idea of human freedom—the assumption of free choice that underlies every move we make, every word we speak, every thought we think. It abolishes the idea of human responsibility, since it is manifestly unfair to reward or punish people for actions that are by definition beyond their control. No one can live consistently by any deterministic creed. The Marxist states prove this themselves by their extreme susceptibility to the cult of leadership.

More than that, history refutes the idea that individuals make no difference. In December 1931 a British politician crossing Fifth Avenue in New York City between 76th and 77th Streets around 10:30 p.m. looked in the wrong direction and was knocked down by an automobile— a moment, he later recalled, of a man aghast, a world aglare: "I do not understand why I was not broken like an eggshell or squashed like a gooseberry." Fourteen months later an American politician, sitting in an open car in Miami, Florida, was fired on by an assassin; the man beside him was hit. Those who believe that individuals make no difference to history might well ponder whether the next two decades would have been the same had Mario Constasino's car killed Winston Churchill in 1931 and Giuseppe Zangara's bullet killed Franklin Roosevelt in 1933. Suppose, in addition, that Lenin had died of typhus in Siberia in 1895 and that Hitler had been killed on the western front in 1916. What would the 20th century have looked like now?

For better or for worse, individuals do make a difference. "The notion that a people can run itself and its affairs anonymously," wrote the philosopher William James, "is now well known to be the silliest of absurdities. Mankind does nothing save through initiatives on the part of inventors, great or small, and imitation by the rest of us—these are the sole factors in human progress. Individuals of genius show the way, and set the patterns, which common people then adopt and follow."

Leadership, James suggests, means leadership in thought as well as in action. In the long run, leaders in thought may well make the greater difference to the world. "The ideas of economists and political philosophers, both when they are right and when they are wrong," wrote John Maynard Keynes, "are more powerful than is commonly understood. Indeed the world is ruled by little else. Practical men, who believe themselves to be quite exempt from any intellectual influences, are usually the slaves of some defunct economist. . . . The power of vested interests is vastly exaggerated compared with the gradual encroachment of ideas."

But, as Woodrow Wilson once said, "Those only are leaders of men, in the general eye, who lead in action. . . . It is at their hands that new thought gets its translation into the crude language of deeds." Leaders in thought often invent in solitude and obscurity, leaving to later generations the tasks of imitation. Leaders in action—the leaders portrayed in this series—have to be effective in their own time.

And they cannot be effective by themselves. They must act in response to the rhythms of their age. Their genius must be adapted, in a phrase from William James, "to the receptivities of the moment." Leaders are useless without followers. "There goes the mob," said the French politician, hearing a clamor in the streets. "I am their leader. I must follow them." Great leaders turn the inchoate emotions of the mob to purposes of their own. They seize on the opportunities of their time, the hopes, fears, frustrations, crises, potentialities. They succeed when events have prepared the way for them, when the community is awaiting to be aroused, when they can provide the clarifying and organizing ideas. Leadership completes the circuit between the individual and the mass and thereby alters history.

It may alter history for better or for worse. Leaders have been responsible for the most extravagant follies and most monstrous crimes that have beset suffering humanity. They have also been vital in such gains as humanity has made in individual freedom, religious and racial tolerance, social justice, and respect for human rights.

There is no sure way to tell in advance who is going to lead for good and who for evil. But a glance at the gallery of men and women in ANCIENT WORLD LEADERS suggests some useful tests.

One test is this: Do leaders lead by force or by persuasion? By command or by consent? Through most of history leadership was exercised by the divine right of authority. The duty of followers was to defer and to obey. "Theirs not to reason why/ Theirs but to do and die." On occasion, as with the so-called enlightened despots of the 18th century in Europe, absolutist leadership was animated by humane purposes. More often, absolutism nourished the passion for domination, land, gold, and conquest and resulted in tyranny.

The great revolution of modern times has been the revolution of equality. "Perhaps no form of government," wrote the British historian James Bryce in his study of the United States, *The American Commonwealth*, "needs great leaders so much as democracy." The idea that all people should be equal in their legal condition has undermined the old structure of authority, hierarchy, and deference. The revolution of equality has had two contrary effects on the nature of leadership. For equality, as Alexis de Tocqueville pointed out in his great study *Democracy in America*, might mean equality in servitude as well as equality in freedom.

"I know of only two methods of establishing equality in the political world," Tocqueville wrote. "Rights must be given to every citizen, or none at all to anyone . . . save one, who is the master of all." There was no middle ground "between the sovereignty of all and the absolute power of one man." In his astonishing prediction of 20th-century totalitarian dictatorship, Tocqueville explained how the revolution of equality could lead to the *Führerprinzip* and more terrible absolutism than the world had ever known.

But when rights are given to every citizen and the sovereignty of all is established, the problem of leadership takes a new form, becomes more exacting than ever before. It is easy to issue commands and enforce them by the rope and the stake, the concentration camp and the *gulag*. It is much harder to use argument and achievement to overcome opposition and win consent. The Founding Fathers of the United States understood the difficulty. They believed that history had given them the opportunity to decide, as Alexander Hamilton wrote in the first Federalist Paper, whether men are indeed capable of basing government on "reflection and choice, or whether they are forever destined to depend . . . on accident and force."

Government by reflection and choice called for a new style of leadership and a new quality of followership. It required leaders to be responsive to popular concerns, and it required followers to be active and informed participants in the process. Democracy does not eliminate emotion from politics; sometimes it fosters demagoguery; but it is confident that, as the greatest of democratic leaders put it, you cannot fool all of the people all of the time. It measures leadership by results and retires those who overreach or falter or fail.

It is true that in the long run despots are measured by results too. But they can postpone the day of judgment, sometimes indefinitely, and in the meantime they can do infinite harm. It is also true that democracy is no guarantee of virtue and intelligence in government, for the voice of the people is not necessarily the voice of God. But democracy, by assuring the right of opposition, offers built-in resistance to the evils inherent in absolutism. As the theologian Reinhold Niebuhr summed it up, "Man's capacity for justice makes democracy possible, but man's inclination to justice makes democracy necessary."

A second test for leadership is the end for which power is sought. When leaders have as their goal the supremacy of a master race or the promotion of totalitarian revolution or the acquisition and exploitation of colonies or the protection of greed and privilege or the preservation of personal power, it is likely that their leadership will do little to advance the cause of humanity. When their goal is the abolition of slavery, the liberation of women, the enlargement of opportunity for the poor and powerless, the extension of equal rights to racial minorities, the defense of the freedoms of expression and opposition, it is likely that their leadership will increase the sum of human liberty and welfare.

Leaders have done great harm to the world. They have also conferred great benefits. You will find both sorts in this series. Even "good" leaders must be regarded with a certain wariness. Leaders are not demigods; they put on their trousers one leg after another just like ordinary mortals. No leader is infallible, and every leader needs to be reminded of this at regular intervals. Irreverence irritates leaders but is their salvation. Unquestioning submission corrupts leaders and demeans followers. Making a cult of a leader is always a mistake. Fortunately, hero worship generates its own antidote. "Every hero," said Emerson, "becomes a bore at last."

The signal benefit the great leaders confer is to embolden the rest of us to live according to our own best selves, to be active, insistent, and resolute in affirming our own sense of things. For great leaders attest to the reality of human freedom against the supposed inevitabilities of history. And they attest to the wisdom and power that may lie within the most unlikely of us, which is why Abraham Lincoln remains the supreme example of great leadership. A great leader, said Emerson, exhibits new possibilities to all humanity. "We feed on genius. . . . Great men exist that there may be greater men."

Great leaders, in short, justify themselves by emancipating and empowering their followers. So humanity struggles to master its destiny, remembering with Alexis de Tocqueville: "It is true that around every man a fatal circle is traced beyond which he cannot pass; but within the wide verge of that circle he is powerful and free; as it is with man, so with communities." ◆

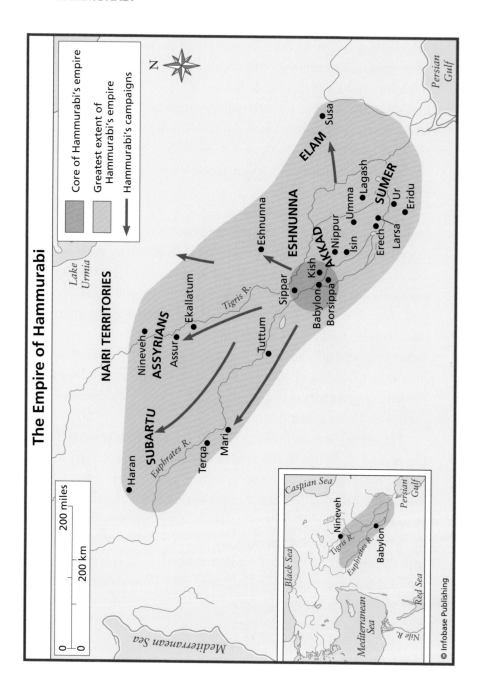

The Empire of Hammurabi

© Infobase Publishing

Hammurabi, King of Justice?

DURING THE WINTER OF 1902–1903, A FRENCH ARCHAEOLOGICAL TEAM was digging up the site of an ancient city named Susa, in what is now Iran, near the border of Iraq. One of their finds would become famous immediately: three large pieces of shiny black stone that formed a monument almost seven and a half feet tall. At the top of the monument was carved the portrait of a man, a king, standing in front of a seated figure, which we now know to be Shamash, the Babylonian god of the sun and also of justice. Below the picture were many rows of writing in the script called cuneiform, meaning "wedge shaped." It is named for the way the writing was usually produced: Scribes pressed a wedge-shaped reed into damp clay. But on this monument, the words were carved very carefully into the black rock.

Scholars had first learned to decipher cuneiform script about 50 years earlier, and in 1902, the French scholar Peré V. Scheil published a complete translation of the inscription. He called it "The Code of Hammurabi." The content of the code was startling to scholars and to ordinary people too. "Hammurabi, King of Babylon," had been one of the names of the ancient Near Eastern kings found inscribed on broken monuments and on crumbling clay tablets dug up from archaeological sites, mostly in what is now Iraq. Scholars had estimated that Hammurabi lived and ruled about 4,000 years ago in the land that the ancient Greeks would later call Mesopotamia, "the land between the rivers"—between the Tigris and the Euphrates.

Hammurabi's laws made him more than just another ancient king. His laws—nearly 300 of them—included ones that said that a person must render "an eye for an eye and a tooth for a tooth." This was the principle of "just retribution" that appears in the Hebrew Bible. Several of Hammurabi's other laws also appear in very similar words in the Bible—except that Hammurabi's code is hundreds of years older. Archaeologists had, they believed, discovered the oldest written code of laws in the world.

On the monument, before and after the list of laws, were passages of writing that sounded almost like poetry. In this prologue and epilogue, translated by M.E.J. Richardson, Hammurabi spoke of the lands he ruled, naming the cities and their gods and temples. He proclaimed that he was "Hammurabi, King of Justice" and that he protected the weak—poor people, widows, orphans—from the powerful. "I have set the people of the land of Sumer and Akkad [old names for southern and northern Mesopotamia] securely on my knees," he said. "They have prospered under my protection. I have made the people lie down in well-watered pastures. I am the shepherd who brings peace."

The Code of Hammurabi is the longest unbroken piece of writing we have from ancient Mesopotamia. It showed that there had been a great king, a lawgiver like the biblical Moses, much earlier than anyone had imagined. Hammurabi's voice spoke out clearly from the monument to the world of 1902 over a distance of nearly 4,000 years. In 1903, more than one book was published comparing Hammurabi to Moses. Hammurabi's reputation in the twentieth century would be based on his description of himself. Even in the 1970s *Chronology of World History*, H.E.L. Mellersh would say of 1792 B.C.: "King Hammurabi the Great establishes the first Babylonian Empire and a golden age of peace, prosperity, and law and order."

IDEALS OF KINGSHIP

As it turns out, fragments of older law codes were excavated and translated in the decades after Hammurabi's was discovered. He was not the first Mesopotamian king to write down a collection of laws, and some of Hammurabi's laws appear in the earlier collections, although his is the longest and—so far—the first mention we have for "an eye for an eye" as a principle of justice. Older laws spoke instead of people paying monetary fines if they injured someone. What is more, archaeologists have found older inscriptions by Mesopotamian kings in which they describe themselves as "shepherds" and speak of the gods giving them the responsibility to protect the weak. So Hammurabi had not thought up these ideas himself. Mesopotamian rulers were supposed to be those things. These ideas were part of the ideals of kingship in Mesopotamia. They were quite distinct from the ideals of an Egyptian king, or pharaoh. The pharaoh was a god, not a shepherd. Still, if Hammurabi was just one of a long line of Mesopotamian kings, why do people continue to study him? Why, nearly 38 centuries after his death, are the first book-length biographies of him being published for adults?

The Code of Hammurabi was written on long cylinders called stela *(above)* and was used in ancient
Mesopotamia as a set of rules decreed by the gods.
Other than Biblical law, Hammurabi's code is the
most comprehensive set of civil, criminal, and family
law from the ancient times.

WHY WE READ ABOUT HAMMURABI

Part of the answer is that the accidents of archaeology have made it possible to study Hammurabi. His law code is one of the most important documents about ancient Babylonian culture that archaeologists have found. Unfortunately, we cannot find out as much about Hammurabi as we would like to. Hammurabi's city of Babylon—the ruins of the city where he lived, where he began his empire—is under the modern water table. That means that when archaeologists try to excavate to the level of 1792–1750 B.C., Hammurabi's reign, any hole they dig just fills up with water. They cannot get to his palace or to his archives.

Still, we do know more about Hammurabi than what he says about himself on his law monument, and scholars have been able to interpret more fully what is written there. Part of what we know is that he was telling the truth when he spoke of the vast regions that he ruled. He inherited a small, not very important city in Babylon, in southern Mesopotamia (about 70 miles south of modern Baghdad) and the realm surrounding it. It had perhaps a radius of 50 miles and included a few other cities. At the end of his reign 43 years later, he ruled the lands stretching from the border of modern Turkey to the Persian Gulf—a land about 700 miles long and 100 miles wide. This was a tremendous achievement. Few other kings had been able to rule over more than a relatively small number of cities in Mesopotamia, and his contemporaries as well as the kings who came after him recognized him as a great and powerful ruler.

Of course, Hammurabi did not gain control of most of Mesopotamia only by being a man of peace and justice. As his law code says, he *pacified* the region. He made war until he ruled all the lands around him and then he had a peaceful land that he could rule justly. He was also a wise and sometimes crafty diplomat. We have letters, reports, and treaties that show him persuading neighboring kings to lend him troops, negotiating deals with other kings in the region (and sometimes playing off one against the other), and managing the demands made upon him by other leaders, by a variety of officials who worked for him, and by the people he ruled.

The Babylonian Empire did not remain unified for very long after Hammurabi died. His son took the throne, and within a decade, local kings again took control of their city-states. Although Hammurabi's dynasty would die out 150 years later, he changed the balance of power in Mesopotamia for long after his death. He was remembered as a king of unusual power and authority. The city of Babylon kept its prestige and remained the greatest city in the region. More than a thousand years after Hammurabi's death, scribes continued to copy his law collection, which helped keep his name alive.

Hittite invaders sacked Babylon in 1595, but as with earlier invaders, the invaders adopted many of the customs and gods of the land they conquered. Not until 539 B.C. did the region finally lose its identity, conquered by a Persian king, Cyrus. Babylonia became part of Persia and never again became an independent region. Yet even after that, Alexander the Great would dream of making Babylon the capital of the whole world.

Hammurabi's law code, his conquest of Mesopotamia, and his own claim to have ruled with justice kept his name alive for 1,200 years after the end of his reign. It was only after a complete conquest of the region by another culture and the end of cuneiform as a way of writing that Hammurabi's name disappeared from memory. But by that time, he and the culture he inherited and passed on would influence much of the world. Mesopotamia, called "the cradle of civilization," was the beginning of Western civilization. It influenced Judaism, Christianity, the ancient Greeks, the ancient Romans—and us, to this day.

HOW WE KNOW WHAT WE KNOW

There is much we do not know about Hammurabi and may never know—so much that it is impossible to write an ordinary biography about him. We do not know when he was born or what his childhood was like. We do not know when or who he married, although one wife at a time was customary for that period and place. Hammurabi's modern biographer, Marc Van De Mieroop, says that it would have been typical for him to inherit the wives of kings he conquered. We know the names of only a few of his children, and those only by chance. We know that there was a daughter who married a neighboring king for diplomatic purposes, to make an alliance between the two cities. (It did not work.) We know the name of the son who became king after him and the name of another son who might have died young because he was the eldest son and should have ruled after Hammurabi but did not. But we do not have letters between Hammurabi and his family, as we do for the king of Mari, for instance, of the same period. The Mari archives were preserved when Hammurabi sacked that city and its palace, while Hammurabi's archives, if they were not looted and destroyed, remain under the water table.

So we know nothing of Hammurabi as a son, a husband, a father. We do not know what he thought or felt about anything. We do know—sometimes—what he did. Generations of historians have pieced together fragments—sometimes literally fragments of broken and crumbled inscribed clay tablets and monuments. We have only a puzzle with missing and broken pieces. From those pieces we construct the story of a leader: A man who came to power in the eighteenth century B.C., and who understood what it meant to lead, well enough to conquer the region and to try to rule it justly. The Babylonian Empire, which began with his reign, lasted 1,200 years. It was an achievement for which the ancients honored him, and we still do.

2

Mesopotamia: "The Cradle of Civilization"

HAMMURABI LIVED SO LONG AGO THAT IT IS DIFFICULT FOR US TO PLACE him in time and space. He lived in what is now Iraq, in a city on the Euphrates River in southern Babylon. And he lived nearly 4,000 years ago. We have to think backward in time to grasp how long ago that was, because it is earlier than almost anything we can think of.

A.D. 1776—The beginning of the United States.

A.D. 1518—Introduction of the fork in France.

A.D. 1492—The discovery by Europeans of what is called the New World.

A.D. 1278—Invention of the glass mirror.

A.D. early 600s—The Prophet Muhammad is born and begins Islam.

A.D. 410—A barbarian tribe called the Goths sacks Rome.

A.D. 221—The Great Wall of China is being built.

A.D. 79—Mount Vesuvius buries the Roman city of Pompeii.

A.D. 43—The Romans invade Great Britain.

45 B.C.—Julius Caesar introduces the modern calendar of 365.25 days with January 1 as the first day of the year.

323 B.C.—Alexander the Great dies in Babylon.

776 B.C.—The first recorded Greek Olympics.

1323 B.C.—The burial of King Tut of Egypt.

1600s B.C.—Egyptians learn to make leavened bread and glass.

1792 B.C.—Hammurabi of Babylon becomes king. His family's dynasty begins about 1894 B.C.

We have to go back very far to get to Hammurabi's era. Before Hammurabi's period, there are a few things we have heard of: The Great Pyramids had been built. The domesticated horse had been introduced in the Near East (though donkeys were still considered more dignified). The camel would not be tamed until 1000 B.C. The chair had been invented (about 2650 B.C., in Egypt), but not pants. We are, in fact, very close to the beginning of history. Not to the beginning of time, obviously, or to the beginning of human beings, but to the part of human existence for which there is *writing*. Not until writing do we have the names of individual people or the names of their cities or of the people's voices speaking to us across time. Before there were written records, archaeologists would name a group of people for the place where they found examples of their pottery or tools, evidence of their early settlements. That is called *pre*history.

THE BEGINNING OF TOWNS

During a relatively short period of prehistory ("short" considering that human beings had been around for at least 100,000 years), people in different parts of the world began to farm crops and domesticate animals. This took place first in Hammurabi's part of the world, in about 10,000 B.C., and then began, independently (they did not learn it from one another), in Egypt, North China, Southeast Asia, central Africa, and North and South America. This change—from hunting animals and gathering wild fruits, vegetables, and grains to growing domesticated crops and raising animals—is the revolution that made towns and then cities possible. More than the discovery of the wheel or any other human invention, farming changed the world. It led to the very beginning of people living in ways that are at all close to anything we would recognize today. We might say "modern." It would also, in the Near East, lead to the beginning of the world's first writing, though not for about another 6,500 years. Writing is the other revolutionary invention that changed human society.

But first, 10,000 B.C.: *Modern* seems a funny word to use about people who could not write yet—and we are now well before Hammurabi's time. But an understanding of this period is necessary to understand the world Hammurabi inherited and the kind of leader he had to be. To understand Hammurabi's Mesopotamia and Hammurabi as a king we have to understand what farming meant in human history.

Historian J.M. Roberts estimates that hunter-gatherers needed thousands of acres to support a family, while the earliest farmers needed perhaps twenty-five. So, farming made it possible for people to remain in one place and build permanent houses. Domesticated crops produce more food than wild ones. It became possible for some people to raise enough food to feed all the people, freeing others to specialize in other activities that did not involve food production. For instance, when archaeologists find the first pottery that looks mass-produced (around 4000 B.C. in the Near East), they are more excited than bored, because it means they have discovered the beginning of pottery made on a potter's wheel by someone whose job it was to make pottery: someone *specialized*. (Also, the potter's wheel is older than wheels on carts and may have given our ancestors the idea of putting wheels on carts in the first place.) It is not until people can specialize that they become experts in building or in crafts that require people to study for many years. Specialists have more time to innovate. Culture would change much faster once people lived in towns and specialized.

What farming peoples could have—for the first time in human existence—was a surplus of food: Enough to feed those people who were making pottery or, later, learning to write. Enough to save and to trade. (The Mesopotamians, for instance, had to trade for wood and stone, because they did not have either. Many of the towns had to trade for metal too.) They had enough to feed more people, so that the size of settlements grew. But these settlements were fragile. It is odd, says Roberts, to speak of "overpopulation" in 4000 B.C., when there were perhaps only about 80 to 85 million people in the whole world; yet the concentration of people in these early towns and then cities made them terribly vulnerable. There was no way to move a lot of food from one place to another and even with food storage, communities were always one drought or one bad harvest away from mass starvation. Social organization became more complex. How was food to be raised, stored, distributed, and defended? (Towns built walls very early as protection.) An important part of the role of the chief, or sheik—the leader or elder of a tribe or extended family group—was to make sure people got fed. The role of the leader and the difficulties of keeping people fed would become more complex as communities consisted of many more people, most of them not related to one another.

THE FERTILE CRESCENT

Until this point it has been possible to talk, generally, about the beginning of agriculture and the way it changed human life. But one of the things we know about settled communities—and the cities some of them became—is that they became more and more different. Their cultures—what people valued and how they felt about the world and what kind of governments and gods they had—differed from place to place and group to group. For instance, Mesopotamia and Egypt produced quite different cultures.

The earliest of the farming cultures—before Egypt or the Indus Valley (in what is now Pakistan) or China or the great civilizations of Mesoamerica (the Incas, Aztecs, and Mayans) or Africa—was in Mesopotamia, near where Hammurabi lived. It is part of the region that American archaeologist James Breasted would, in 1916, name "The fertile crescent": A curved area of plains that begins up in modern Turkey and reaches south through modern Iraq and Iran and down to Syria and Egypt. It is not, by and large, an area that we now think of as having great fertility. But the Tigris and Euphrates rivers had deposited large amounts of fertile soil near where they emptied into the Arabian Gulf. That was about 200 miles inland from what is now the shore: The ancient city of Ur was a seafront city when it was built. Still, in both southern Mesopotamia and Egypt, the fertility of the land was based entirely on the people's relationship to rivers, on their ability to harness the rivers and use them for irrigation. But the rivers they were working with had very different habits and were, at least, in part responsible for the different cultures that developed in the two regions.

Throughout the centuries, climate changes and excessive damming have altered most of the Middle East from lush landscape to desert. The ancient Sumerian city of Ur, for example, was established years ago by the sea but is now surrounded by sand *(above)*.

The Nile River flooded once a year, after the harvest, just in time to lay down a rich bed of fertile soil in which to plant the new crops. It was a reliable river (more or less), and the Egyptians considered it a friend and also a god. Irrigation was a matter of making sure water was guided toward the crops as they grew. Neither Egypt nor southern Mesopotamia had enough rainfall to grow crops without irrigation. In Egypt, towns grew up all along the Nile. The river made possible a narrow band of farming along its whole length. The towns did not become cities and they did not become separate from one another or (usually) do battle among one another. Egypt was a united kingdom by 3000 B.C., although it did not always stay united.

The Tigris and Euphrates rivers were less "considerate" than the Nile, if we can use that word about a river. The Euphrates was slower moving, and the earliest farming communities grew up along it, rather than along the speedier Tigris, but neither was easy to tame. Both these rivers flooded every year at a time when the crops were not yet harvested and would destroy them. People living along these rivers (which changed course periodically, making it necessary for the towns to move) had to contain the river and protect their fields from floods. They banked their fields (and the river) and built canals to contain the surplus water, and then they irrigated from these canals. (They would also use the river and canals for transportation.) This is harder than what the Egyptians had to do. One family or even a small group of families could not do the work necessary to harness the Tigris or Euphrates. People had to work together in larger groups. Instead of continuous cultivation along the rivers, as in Egypt, what grew up were separate towns, then city-states. A city-state was a large group of people living together and the outlying fields and smaller towns that surrounded it. Land that could be cultivated was valuable and hard to care for, so shepherds grazed animals in marginal areas where crops could not be grown. These were probably first organized around a temple or shrine, which could store grains. Some of the city-states would grow, and their leaders would, in time, become more powerful.

That kind of settlement, the city-state rather than the village, became the basic structure of Mesopotamia: walled, separate cities that did not form a country and were nearly always in conflict with one another for scarce resources. At the same time, the need for people to work together and the need to import resources like wood and stone seem to have encouraged some extremely interesting developments in human culture. Trade was one of these. The first writing on earth was another. Writing was developed by a Mesopotamian people who remained entirely unknown to scholars until the nineteenth century: the Sumerians.

HISTORY BEGINS AT SUMER

In 1959, archaeologist and historian Samuel Noah Kramer published a book called *History Begins at Sumer*. In it, he chronicles a series of "firsts" in human history, all of them in Sumer, in what would become southern Mesopotamia. These included the first written literature, the first written law code (older even than Hammurabi's), the first written myths about how the world began, the first story of a great flood that destroys the world (much like the biblical Noah and his ark).

The Sumerian people are one of the great mysteries of human history. No one knows who they were or where they came from. It is not clear if they migrated to southern Mesopotamia or if their culture developed out of the prehistoric peoples already living in that region. The Sumerian language is related to no other language on earth, living or dead. Although it would come to coexist with the Babylonian that Hammurabi spoke, which was a version of the Akkadian language spoken in northern Mesopotamia, the languages are in no way related. They are not just as different as, say, English and French are different, but as the French and Chinese languages are different. Akkadian (it is named for the ancient city of Akkad, which was somewhere in the north of Mesopotamia) is a Semitic language, which means it is related to modern Arabic and Hebrew. And Sumerian is related to nothing. Nevertheless, the peoples of Mesopotamia would keep it as their written language for many centuries, as they would keep much of Sumerian civilization: its gods, its literature, its beliefs about kingship, and its record keeping, in cuneiform script.

THE DISCOVERY OF SUMER

Until the middle 1900s, no one knew the Sumerians ever existed. No one could read their cuneiform script and there are no references to the Sumerians in the writings of the ancient Greeks and Romans or in the Bible, which were the sources of knowledge in the ancient world. People knew the Greeks and Romans. People knew about the ancient Egyptians—they are in the Bible and they left huge monuments—although research about the ancient Egyptians started when Napoléon sent historians and archaeologists to Egypt in the late 1700s. Hieroglyphics were completely deciphered by 1822 because the Rosetta Stone was discovered. On it is inscribed the same text in three languages, including hieroglyphics and Greek, which people already knew how to read.

The Near East was exciting to people because it is the land of the Bible, but (unlike in Egypt) there was not much to see. The Mesopotamians, building with brick, not stone, created more fragile buildings. As these crumbled, they would be knocked down and new ones built on top of them. So the sites of older abandoned cities formed hills, called tells, but these were not as exciting as pyramids. They just looked like piles of broken bricks. Still, a map from the early 1600s shows the Garden of Eden to be in Mesopotamia because the Bible says it was located between the Tigris and Euphrates rivers.

Cuneiform would be more complicated to interpret than hieroglyphics had been. Archaeologist Austen Henry Layard, responsible for many important discoveries in the Near East, described cuneiform tablets as "bits of pottery decorated in an unusual manner," in Leo Deuel's *Treasures of Time*. Earlier scholars had said the markings looked like "bird tracks on wet sand." No one even recognized it as a writing system. But when George Smith interpreted an ancient Mesopotamian account of the flood in 1872 and then identified an equally ancient Genesis in 1875, the discoveries rocked the world. Even before the discovery of Hammurabi's code and its similarity to the Hebrew Bible, they had cuneiform texts that sounded a lot like the Bible, but were written much earlier. This was not just a matter of scholarly interest. The London *Daily Telegraph* newspaper published the news. Author Karen Rhea Nemet-Nejat stated that Smith, working in the British Museum, was "so excited that he ran around the room removing his clothes, much to the aston-ishment of his colleagues in the department."

Then, between 1922 and 1934, British archaeologist Leon-ard Woolley excavated part of the Sumerian city of Ur and unearthed city streets, a palace, and royal tombs filled with gold and with the dead bodies of a king and his servants. (This does not seem to have become a regular feature of burials in that region. Hammurabi would not have been buried like that.) In the Hebrew Bible, Abraham comes from the city of Ur. Wool-ley believed he had discovered proof of the historical reality of Abraham (this remains hotly debated) and also of Noah's flood. (This also remains debatable. Woolley believed there was one huge flood. Since then, archaeologists have discovered evidence of flooding at different levels—different times of prehistory—which means there were many smaller floods, not one big one.) But needless to say, this all made the Sumerians and all of Near Eastern archaeology very exciting indeed.

HOW WRITING BEGAN

Why did so much begin with the Sumerians? One partial answer is that the high degree of social cooperation required to farm there led to a need for record keeping, and that record keeping seems to have led to the first writing. The Sumerians did not begin by writing down their myths or literature: They (or perhaps the people who came before them) began by keep-ing track of collections and deliveries of products like oil, wheat, and sheep.

According to Denise Schmandt-Besserat, scholar of Middle Eastern studies, before there was writing, there was a system of clay tokens. As early as 8500 B.C., small clay pieces in different shapes—spheres, cones, disks, and other shapes—were used to count measures of oil or quantities of grain. About 3500 B.C., at the time of the first cities, these tokens began to be inserted into sphere-shaped clay "envelopes." On the outside of some of these envelopes, while the clay was still soft, people pressed the tokens. This showed what was inside. But once this had been done, there was no real use for the tokens themselves anymore: All the information necessary had been recorded on the envelope. This was not writing yet, because it was so limited. A real writing system can record what people say—their actual words and grammar—so that someone else can read their words. But the idea that something can be pressed into soft clay and leave a message is the beginning of writing.

Also, cylinder seals were used in the Near East as a kind of signature, before the invention of writing. A person would have an individual seal with a picture on it, often of animals, agricultural products, or people. Rolling the seal on wet clay, sometimes on a clay envelope, would leave a mark that meant "this is mine" or "this is from me." It was like when we sign a document: Our signature means more than just our name.

With the clay tokens, the ancient peoples of the Near East were able to keep (and send) detailed records of transactions involving livestock, grain, and other objects. They also recorded land ownership and transfers. These were matters of great importance, and, Schmandt-Besserat argues, account for the earliest form of writing in the world. Once the transition had been made to impressing the tokens in the soft clay envelopes, it was not long until people began to carve symbols—pictographs standing for words or ideas—in clay. As symbols began to stand for sounds and could thus reproduce speech, they would become the first real writing.

The Sumerians would continue to be great record keepers and list makers, carrying into their writing their concerns with administration—taxes, tributes, the collection and distribution of goods. They would also begin to compile lists: all the known kinds of trees or fish, all the literary tablets in an archive (like a library catalog), and all the kings that had ever been. They made lists of all the words they knew, which may have been used in the schools where scribes were taught.

The cylinder seal, used as a signature, was an early form of written identification. The cylinders were carved with special designs and pressed on wet, soft clay to create a personal marker. Cylinders usually depicted agriculture or animals, or sometimes even battles between men and mythical creatures (above).

Cuneiform would spread to Akkad in the north and be used to write their very different language. It would also be used (for over a thousand years) to write other languages as well. Egyptian hieroglyphics were probably inspired by cuneiform.

The Sumerians are the first people who left us their words, and so we can know what they thought about their world and what they said to one another. We can read their mail. We have their records of how they taught one another to plant a field or heal a wound. We can read about how they thought the world began and what they called their gods. They are the first people we can see struggling with the questions that continue to plague human beings: Where did we come from? Why do people have to die? And although they were not writing history, things they

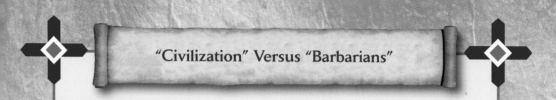

"Civilization" Versus "Barbarians"

Writing about the beginning of civilization, we sometimes take for granted that it is "better" to live in houses and grow crops (or have someone do it for us) than to live like those hunting and gathering peoples. That attitude has had major consequences in world history: Europeans believed it was right to displace tribal peoples in North and South America.

These attitudes existed in ancient Mesopotamia. There were peoples living outside the city-states—nomads who did not grow crops, although they did herd animals. The Sumerians said that they were barbarians who ate their meat raw and did not bury their dead, serve the gods, live in houses, or "know grain." The nomadic/tribal peoples of the Near East were often a problem for the cities. The tribal peoples would sometimes invade—but the city-states did the same to one another.

Yet these tribal peoples also moved into the cities over the years and adopted city ways. Some became kings. Even as nomads, they were not as "wild" as city people imagined. In those days without camels, they could not go far. Many had a place where they lived much of the year. They moved their animals (and animals belonging to the city people) to winter and summer pastures. They lived organized lives, bound by laws and responsibilities.

It is true that civilization as we know it—urban, literate, bureaucratic—first existed in the ancient Near East, so we can look to them as our earliest cultural ancestors. Still, the peoples who settled in cities were making a choice about how to live and other people made other choices. Tribal peoples have produced complex and beautiful artworks, as well as caring for people who could not collect food for themselves. So, although the concept of the "cradle of civilization" is exciting, we should not lose sight of how wrong—or brutal—"civilized" peoples have been to tribal ones.

wrote tell us about their history: a list of kings, laws, instructions on how to plan a battle, the poetry that was written when a city was invaded.

THE PEOPLE AND THE GODS

The history we need to know to understand Hammurabi and his world begins very early. It begins with the need to organize people so that the land can be farmed efficiently. That means the land must not be flooded or dried out. It must not be over-used. Irrigation made the earth salty, because the water used was slightly salty. Farmers had to rest fields every four years and sometimes plant barley rather than wheat, because barley can grow in saltier soil. The canals that brought water to the fields needed to be kept cleared. More had to be built as populations grew and more fields to farm were needed. Farmers needed to bank their fields and not let the water overflow into a neighbor's fields. Food was collected and distributed.

Some of the writings found are very modern and scientific sounding: A "farmer's almanac" describes how to prepare a field for planting and how to plant it. There is a letter in which a king tells his wife that a woman in the palace who has a contagious disease must be kept in quarantine, and that others must not drink from her glass so that her disease will not be spread. We also have thousands of documents about the distribution, sale, and renting of land, about taxes and tribute and soldiers.

All of this sounds reasonably modern. We can easily under-stand irrigation and taxes and land rental, and we can imagine how complex life was for people who were first figuring out how to handle these matters. They were good at it too. Yet it is equally impossible to understand Hammurabi and his world with-out understanding that for the peoples of the Near East, their observable world was inseparable from the world of the gods. The historian J.M. Roberts says that their world was fragile and delicately balanced because the density of the population could easily outstrip the resources available to feed them. The ancient Mesopotamians would have agreed. But they would also have said that the world was fragile and delicately balanced because you really never knew what the gods were going to do next. "You cannot teach your god to run like a dog after you," said a Sumerian proverb.

So here is the part of the Mesopotamian culture that does not sound modern: The Mesopotamian peoples understood themselves to be living on a flat disk of land floating on the fresh waters of the deep. Those waters broke through the surface in the form of rivers or groundwater (what one reaches when digging a well) or as marshes. Above the world was a solid sky shaped like an inverted bowl, possibly made of tin. Below was the netherworld, where people went when they died. All around was "bitter water"—the ocean.

What do we make of the part of this culture that attributed the downfall of cities to disrespecting the gods, who believed that a king or general should have the diviners read the liver of a sheep for him to know when he should invade a city? What do we need to understand about their myths? A common meaning of "myth" confuses the matter, because we use the word to mean something that is untrue—a false belief. That use of the word is very old: The Greek philosopher Plato, writing in the early fourth century B.C., described mythic thinking as the opposite of rational thinking. As he saw it, a myth is a kind of antiscientific thinking that uses stories to explain things that would better be explained by science and history. To this way of thinking, ancient (or "primitive") people are not advanced enough for science, so they make up stories instead.

But the persistence of religion and, perhaps, of literature, suggests another explanation: There seem to be things in human experience that we continue to explain through stories and symbolism. We struggle still to understand mortality, loss, and the

By impressing a series of wedge-shaped lines onto wet clay, early Sumerians were able to document their daily lives using cuneiform. Mundane events like hitching donkeys to a plow were recorded on tablets *(above)* in cuneiform. These artifacts allow archaeologists and researchers to understand the habits and customs of ancient life.

tendency of life to send us very odd experiences indeed. Where did we come from? Why do people have to work so hard? Why do bad things happen to good people? What are we doing here? Hammurabi and the people who came before him asked these questions and tried to answer them.

For instance, they said that after An, the god of the sky, created the world, some less powerful gods had the job of planting food and digging canals and all the other back-breaking work that people in Mesopotamia had to do. The worker-gods got tired of it and complained to Enlil, the god of wind, one of the three highest gods and the patron god of Sumer. Ea, the god of fresh water, created humans beings to do the work instead, and they inherited the responsibility to feed and care for the gods. Thus the Mesopotamian temple was like an elegant house for a very important guest. In fact, the word for temple was the same as the word for house. The god—and each city had one special god who was in charge of it, their patron god—had to be fed wonderful meals and given beautiful furniture. The king had the main responsibility to see that these duties were carried out. There were thousands of gods and they fought with one another like people fight (and as the Greek and Roman gods would fight) and fell in love and generally behaved like immortal humans, and people often landed in the fallout of their arguments. The patron god was meant to keep an eye out for them. In exchange for their loyalty and devotion this patron god would (they hoped) look out for the city, make its harvests plentiful, and help keep it safe.

We can look at myths to understand better how the people in a culture—people sharing certain values and beliefs and ways of doing things—understood themselves and their world. Much of human experience is shared everywhere: People are born and die and they wonder what happens to people after death; they note the rising of the sun in the morning and the stars overhead at night. Most mythologies address these matters, but do not come to the same conclusion. The Egyptians believed in an afterlife to which people can bring their treasures and live again, rather happily. The Mesopotamian peoples believed in a dark and gloomy afterlife, where people ate dust in dark and silence. Theirs was a difficult and sad afterlife and, in many ways, an insecure, nervous, and gloomy mythology. It is possible to understand this as a reflection of their lives: The ancient Sumerians and Akkadians lived with those fierce, difficult rivers, the constant tensions between city-states and raids from nomads and other peoples. It was even a difficult landscape—flat, treeless, brutally hot and dry, punctuated by windstorms, floods, and drought. It was a culture whose natural resources were mud and ingenuity, and not much else. They were born to labor, they believed, and at the mercy of forces they could not control.

The Mesopotamians saw the will (or whim) of gods in nearly everything. Yet, in a culture for which writing was still new and exciting, they saw a world in which the gods could "write" messages to them. The diviners who read oracles—who looked for messages from the gods in the liver of sheep, who read the meaning of dreams, or made predictions based on unusual events (the birth of twins or of a deformed child, an unusual weather pattern)—were looking for messages written by the gods. This knowledge did not replace other ways of making decisions, but it supplemented it. The king knew to isolate a woman with a contagious disease, farmers knew that there was a right way and a wrong way to prepare a field for sowing, and kings and generals made decisions based on their experience and what their spies told them, not only on what the oracles said. They observed the world carefully and made scientific, mathematical, medical, and astronomical observations. If a king was a successful diplomat, it was because he was good at persuading people to help him and clever at underrstanding what his enemies were likely to do.

But the gods were everywhere, and only they gave a king the right to rule.

3

The Land of Sumer and Akkad

HAMMURABI'S FAMILY WERE AMORITES, A SEMITIC NOMADIC PEOPLE FROM the west. Along with the Elamites, (from what is now Iran) they conquered many of the Sumerian cities in about 2000 B.C. And yet, as had happened before in Mesopotamia, the invaders then settled in and adopted Sumerian culture almost entirely, including the concept of kingship that had developed. The spoken language would change, but scribes would continue to learn and write in Sumerian.

Even before the Amorite and Elamite invasion, Sumer (in the south of Mesopotamia) and Akkad (in the north) had not been united or peaceful. Hammurabi inherited a world in which power struggles and changes of administration had occurred often.

THE BEGINNING OF KINGS

Sumer began in prehistory, perhaps in the fourth millennium B.C. The Sumerians believed it began several hundred thousand years earlier. There are records called the Sumerian King List, written early in the second millennium B.C. The list begins in mythic, prehistoric times, with rulers who each reigned for tens of thousands of years. The list says, "After the kingship descended from heaven, the kingship was in Eridu [an ancient real city]. In Eridu, Alulim became king; he ruled for 28,800 years." (The Sumerian counting system was based on units of 60, so those early kings ruled for multiples of 60. We inherited the Sumerian counting system in our 60-minute hour and 360 degree circle.)

Then Ea, who had created humans, kept awake by all the noise people were making, sent the flood. Only Ziusudra was warned to build a big ship and save some people and animals to repopulate the earth. (After all, the myth says, the gods did not want to go back to having to farm and dig canals.) "After the flood had swept over the land, and the kingship had descended from heaven, the kingship was in Kish [another real city]," says the King List. The kings who reigned after the flood were supposed to have lived for hundreds of years each. The list's greatest problem as a historical tool is that the Sumerians wrote it as though there was only one real king at a time. So they will say that a dynasty and city were defeated and then the kingship went to a different city, while in fact, many kings ruled at the same time, in different cities. The Sumerians were not a country with one king but a series of separate city-states that shared a language and a culture.

Between about 3360 and 2400 B.C., local dynasties grew stronger and kings (who in Sumerian were simply called "Big Men") grew more powerful. Priests and more representative governments grew less powerful. Kingship grew up in the larger, more important, more complex cities. In times of war, power would be centralized in one man, but it gradually became a more permanent role passed from father to son (or sometimes brother). As the King List shows, kingship was understood as "descending from heaven." The gods made someone king, but the king was also answerable to the gods.

As early as 2500 B.C., there are inscriptions and art that show how the idea of kingship was developing. King Ur-nanshe of the city of Lagash is portrayed on a stone plaque carrying a basket on his head, demonstrating that he is fulfilling his responsibility to build and maintain a temple for the gods. Inscriptions explain that this is his duty. By keeping the god's help and blessings, he ensures that there is plenty for his people. King Ur-nanshe also digs canals, builds city walls, and trades for timber from far away. Another king, Ur-Uinimagina, describes himself as the "righter of wrongs and defender of the weak." So, from as early as we have records of what kingship meant, the Sumerian kings were protectors of their people and servants to the gods. They were not, as in Egypt, gods themselves.

SARGON THE GREAT

The first break in Sumerian rule came with the conquest and unification of Sumer by a northern Semitic king named Sargon in about 2334 B.C. Sargon founded the city of Akkad and he ruled for 40 years. Though its location is unknown, its name would be used to refer to northern Mesopotamia long after the city was gone. From that time on, the region was "the lands of Sumer and Akkad" and the northern people were Akkadians. And yet this was not the end of Sumerian civilization but only a phase in its history. Sargon did not end Sumerian culture but instead added to it. He began the custom of giving "year names" as a dating system and began keeping a royal archive, where written tablets were filed.

Sargon was a real king and also a character about whom legends would be told. His name means "legitimate king," which

The king of Lagash, Ur-Nanshe, is depicted on this stone tablet *(left)*, carrying a basket of bricks for the building of a temple. As king, it was Ur-Nanshe's responsibility to respect and honor the gods by constructing a grand temple, a gesture that ensures good fortune for his subjects.

means he was not one, in the sense of having inherited the king-ship from his father. The King List said that Sargon was the son of a gardener who became cupbearer to King Ur-Zababa and inherited the kingship from him. Other stories said that he was the son of a temple priestess who was forbidden to bear a child and so sealed the baby in a basket and set him in the river to be rescued, as would later be said of the biblical Moses. King Ur-Zababa was a good king, a mighty king, so strong that he had "5,400 soldiers eating before him in his palace." His soldiers were the first full-time army in the region. That made the king very strong indeed, and he was the first of several empire-building Semitic kings who would overpower and unite the region. Much later, Hammurabi would be another.

For all Sargon's power, Akkad was not a capital city and the region was not a country. He tore down city walls and replaced local rulers who would not swear allegiance to him. He collected tribute (taxes in the form of goods), but there still was no idea of (or mechanism for) creating a nation in Mesopotamia. People still described themselves as belonging to a particular city.

THE FALL OF AKKAD

Two of Sargon's sons ruled after him and maintained his kingdom. By the time his grandson, Naram-Sin, was king, the dynasty was immensely powerful and the idea of kingship had changed somewhat. King Naram-Sin was one of the few Mesopotamian kings to call himself a god. He was "god of Agade" and "King of the Four Quarters." A stela (tall monument) of one of his military victories shows him wearing a horned helmet, trampling a tall pile of dead or dying enemies. In earlier (and later) pictures or sculpture, that horned helmet always meant that the figure wearing it was a god.

Although Naram-Sin would rule the lands of Sumer and Akkad for 56 years and be succeeded by his son, later legends said that the fall of Sargon's empire was his grandson's fault. Then and now the fall of the empire can be seen as a lesson for all of what could go wrong for a Mesopotamian ruler. The legend said that Naram-Sin stole statues and other sacred items from the temple in the city of Nippur. The temple belonged to Enlil, "Lord Wind," the head god of all of Sumer, and so the gods cursed Akkad. The curse took the form of a famine. Then, people from the Gutian tribe were able to invade the weakened city. And so, the fall of the city could be understood to have "natural" causes, but to the Akkadians and Sumerians, it began with the failure of the king to respect the gods.

A somewhat later Sumerian hymn (a poem that was sung) called "The Curse of Akkad," describes the sacking of Nippur and the destruction of Enlil's temple. It shows us, vividly, what it meant for a city to be cursed, and it also shows us the opposite. It tells us what the people of that time thought a thriving, healthy city should be like. In the cursed city, the canal towpaths and the city roads are covered with weeds and inhabited by "wild goats, vermin, snakes, and mountain scorpions." So, things that are wild and dangerous have invaded what should be safe and a source of prosperity. Without canals and roads, trade and communications are impossible. In a cursed city, the poem says, the river is "bitter" (salty) instead of "sweet" and so it is undrinkable and cannot be used for irrigation. Nothing edible grows in the fields. A city in which these things have happened would indeed feel it had been cursed: Nothing is what it should be. People begin to starve. It is that system of canals, roads, fruitful fields, and keeping the wild and dangerous things away that make life possible.

The Sumerian King List becomes almost plaintive at this point. It interrupts its list of names to ask, "Who was the king? Who was not the king?" A world without a legitimate king, a king given power by the gods, is a world in chaos. Although certainly some cities had rulers (remember that the King List considers there to be only one real king at a time while in reality there were many), it would have been a time of great insecurity.

After a period of instability, King Gudea, another Sumerian ruler, came to the throne of the city of Lagash. There is a statue of King Gudea holding the plans for a temple that a god revealed to him in a dream. The inscription says he built it, importing gold and silver, red stone, "cedars from the Cedar Mountains, pines from the Pine Mountains." Here again is a man who knew how to be a leader.

THE THIRD DYNASTY OF UR

For about a century, a series of powerful Sumerian kings ruled. King Ur-Nammu controlled a number of the old, important

Sumerian cities, including Ur, Eridu, Uruk, and other southern cities. He began the building of a huge ziggurat at Ur. A ziggurat looks rather like an Egyptian pyramid with steps, but is quite different. A pyramid contained a burial. A ziggurat was solid, would have been brightly painted, and had a temple on its top. It was an attempt to reach toward the gods, to put a god's temple as close to the sky as possible. The biblical "Tower of Babel" was a ziggurat, though it was built much later, and its name was a play on words. "Bab-ilim," the Akkadian language's name for what we call Babylon, meant "gate of god." The Hebrew (Babil) means "confusion."

Ur-Nammu's son, Shulgi, ruled for 46 years and once again began to unite the lands of Akkad and Sumer. In Shulgi we can see an ideal of kingship that is both related to what came before and also to the one that Hammurabi would inherit. Shulgi created a law code to establish justice in the land. He reinforced the city walls and built a wall along the kingdom's northwest border to keep out the Amorite tribes. He had the first army that had specialized units—a unit of spearmen, for one. There is a royal hymn about Shulgi that explains all the ways he was a wonderful king. Although they are written in the king's voice—"I did all these things" the singer says—they were not written by or sung by the king. They were sung about him. As "The Curse of Akkade" shows us what a city should and should not be, a royal hymn shows us what an ideal king should be.

The highest gods appointed Shulgi, says the hymn. He is a perfect soldier and commander, so strong and brave and clever at handling weapons that he terrifies his enemies. He takes care of the temples and so makes the land prosper. He dispenses justice and protects the weak. The king is also wise and learned, says the hymn. He can read and write (perhaps, but it took scribes from childhood to adulthood to master the difficulties of cuneiform), could add and subtract, could speak five languages, and could read omens (again a rare and highly skilled craft). He could play *every* musical instrument, including one

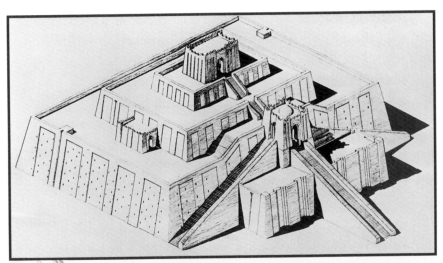

In honor of the god Sin, King Ur-Nammu built a giant ziggurat in the city Ur. Called "Etemennigur," which means "House whose foundation creates terror," Ur-Nammu constructed a colorful temple on the highest terrace using glazed bricks. The first stage of the ziggurat was built with 720,000 clay bricks, each stamped with Ur-Nammu's name and title.

so ancient that no one knows what it is anymore. Also, he is good-looking—and he fights his lions face-to-face. (Only the king is allowed to kill a lion. A later king, a neighbor of Hammurabi's, will have a lion mailed to him in a cage because it was on someone's roof, and the king's official cannot get it to eat and is afraid it will die.) So Shulgi faces the danger of the lion rather than hide in a pit and capture it in a net, which is an easier, if less glorious, way to kill one.

The hymn lists many more of Shulgi's virtues and skills, which include his having improved the roads and footpaths of the land. He is also a champion runner of great distances (he does not even get tired). In among the claims are the real virtues of a king and the real Shulgi seems to have been a good one, completing the ziggurat his father started, founding and supporting two scribal schools, and standardizing the weights and measures of the land. And, unlike Naram-Sin, he was reverent to the gods.

LAMENT FOR UR

At the end of the third dynasty of Ur, 42 years after the end of Shulgi's reign, Ur—and the Sumerians—fell. Again an empire collapsed as local kings took back control of their cities and tribal peoples—this time the Amorites—invaded (or perhaps had already moved into the city). As had often happened (and would again), the descendent of a great ruler would be able to maintain power only in his own city, this time the ancient city of Ur. Then, around 2004 B.C., the people called Elamites (from a region Shulgi had ruled for a time, in what is now Iran) sacked and plundered the ancient city of Ur.

There was in Mesopotamia a kind of hymn about the destruction of a city. Cities were destroyed so often that the hymns have a name: the city lament. In them we can hear the voices of an ancient people brought to their knees with pain, suffering, and regret for their lost home. The city laments are long, but these are short portions of two of them.

> From "Lamentation over the Destruction of Sumer and Ur":
> Hunger filled the city like water, it would not cease.
> This hunger contorts people's faces, it twists their muscles.
> Its people are as if surrounded by water, they gasp for breath.
> Its king breathed heavily in his palace, all alone.
>
> —Amélie Kuhrt, *The Ancient Near East, c. 3000–330 BC*

> From "Lamentation over the Destruction of Ur":
> In all the streets and roadways bodies lay.
> In open fields that used to fill with dancers, they lay in heaps.
> The country's blood now filled its holes, like metal in a mold;
> Bodies dissolved—like fat left in the sun.
>
> —Thorkild Jacobsen's *The Harps That Once . . .*
> *Sumerian Poetry in Translation.*)

These are horrible images: starvation, no one left to bury the dead, places of celebration full of corpses. "The very foundation of Sumer was torn out," says the Sumerian King List. This time there was no suggestion, as with Akkad, that a king's misdeeds had caused the city's downfall. Instead, the lament said Sumer had exhausted itself, it had just worn out over all those years. They would have said hundreds of thousands of years. We would say, from about 3300 to 2000 B.C., beginning with the first Sumerian writing and ending with the fall of Ur.

Although Ur fell and the Sumerians were defeated, the civilization that they had created would live on in their conquerors. New kings, Amorites, came to rule the cities of Isin and Larsa— and in about 1894 B.C., another Amorite ruler took the throne of a small city called Babel, or Babylon. Author J.N. Postgate states that the Sumerians said the Amorites were "a ravaging people, with the instincts of a beast." Hammurabi was the sixth of that dynasty of Amorite kings. Despite the Sumerian's rude remarks about raw-meat-eating barbarians and the genuine horror of the fall of cities, the Amorite kings would be absorbed by their cities and its culture and rule very much as kings had ruled in that part of the world for over 1,000 years.

4

Hammurabi: Sixth in a Dynasty of Invaders

BY THE TIME HAMMURABI INHERITED THE KINGSHIP OF BABYLON FROM his father, Sin-muballit, in 1792 B.C., the family's dynasty was well established. No one would have questioned his right to be king.

We know nothing of Hammurabi's childhood or even how old he was when he became king. If he was his parent's oldest son, he would have grown up knowing that he would rule. Even if he had an older brother who died, he might still have been prepared to rule: Mesopotamian kings did sometimes pass the kingship from brother to brother. In any event, he would have been raised to know what it meant to be a king, and he would have understood the specific political situation that existed at that time. Since the fall of Ur there was (as there had often been) an uneasy balance of power among the regional kings and other rulers. It is useful to remember, though, that although we speak of the end of the Sumerians, their language was still used for writing, as Latin was in the Middle Ages and the Renaissance. The world the Sumerians had created—a literate, bureaucratic network of city-states including farmers, craftspeople, slaves, priests, merchants, and administrators—remained.

The Babylon that Hammurabi inherited was small in comparison to some of his neighbors' kingdoms. Hammurabi's family ruled over the nearby cities of Kish, Sippar, and Borsippa. This explains how he ruled for the first 30 years he was king: quietly.

REGIONAL POWERS

To Hammurabi's south was one of the region's strongest kingdoms. King Rim-Sin of Larsa, an old king who had already ruled for many years, controlled much of central and southern Mesopotamia. He had, when Hammurabi took the throne, only recently conquered the city of Isin, which had become the most important central Mesopotamian city after the fall of Ur. Rim-Sin had no reason to trust or like Hammurabi, whose father had sided with Rim-Sin's enemies in 1810 B.C.

Another power—one that would become critical later in Hammurabi's reign—was the region called Elam, just outside of what we traditionally call Mesopotamia, because it was not between the Tigris and the Euphrates rivers. It lay to the east of the Tigris, in what is now Iran, toward the Zagros Mountains. Its capital, Susa, had been founded in the fourth millennium B.C. The territory was ruled by a man who carried the title *sukkalmah*—supreme leader—and who had under him men called *sukkal*. The sukkalmah when Hammurabi became king was named Siwe-palar-huppak. Elam was important to Hammurabi and the other kings of the time because it lay on a major trade route to what are now eastern Iran and Afghanistan. They needed to import copper and tin to create bronze in order to make tools and weapons. Bronze was the only metal they had that was hard enough to take an edge, iron not yet being in use. They also traded for the blue semiprecious stone called lapis lazuli, which they used to make jewelry and to decorate beautiful items for the temples. Elam was also a key source of wood and stone, neither of which existed in southern Mesopotamia.

During this period, Elam had a special relationship with the Mesopotamian city-states. The Sukkalmah of Elam did not interfere with them. He did not try to conquer them or collect tribute from them, although all of the regional leaders exchanged gifts and met with one another's representatives in order to cement relations and try to keep on a good footing with one another. Still, the Sukkalmah of Elam was accepted as a sort of higher authority. In the letters that the leaders sent one another during this time, Hammurabi and the other kings called the sukkalmah "father" and one another "brother." One is a relationship of subordination, the other of equality.

To the northeast was another powerful region, the state of Eshnunna. The city was on the Tigris River and was also important because of trade routes.

THE REGION'S GREATEST POWER

Perhaps the most powerful of the kings was the man who had united upper Mesopotamia, Shamshi-Adad. He was from a family of outsiders—like Hammurabi, from the Amorites. In the 1800s, Shamshi-Adad inherited the throne from his father and expanded his empire. His older son, Ishme-Dagan, represented his father in Ekallatum on the Tigris. Then, in 1796 B.C., just before Hammurabi became king, Shamshi-Adad took over the ancient city of Mari and installed his younger son, Yasmah-Addu, as the local ruler there.

Because the royal archives at Mari are especially well preserved, we have records of many of the political dealings among the rulers of the time. We also have some of the very detailed

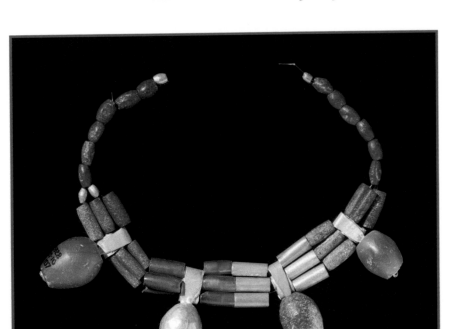

The materials needed in Hammurabi's kingdom were abundant in the region of Elam. A trade route that ran through the area added to the power of the kingdom, whose lands provided wood, metals, and stone to Mesopotamia. One of the most valued Elamite resources, a blue semi-precious stone called lapis lazuli, was popularly used for decoration, such as the Ur civilization jewelry (*above*).

instructions that Shamshi-Adad gave his sons about how to rule their cities or fight a battle.

Additionally, we have some letters that bring these ancient kings and their world to life, and these are valuable because these people otherwise seem so distant. They can seem like names and dates and not people at all. From the midst of unfamiliar, strange-sounding names, we hear a powerful empire-building king, exasperated with his incompetent younger son and that son's reply. It also reminds us what it meant to write a letter then. The kings could not read or write. Very few people could. So, the person sending the letter spoke to a scribe who inscribed it on a clay tablet, and then, when the letter was received, another scribe read it out. Author Amélie Kuhrt cites surely one of the earliest records of hurt feelings that have been found:

> Speak to Daddy: thus speaks Yasmah-Addu, your son. I listened to the tablet Daddy sent me, which ran as follows: "How much longer do we have to keep you on a leading rein? You are a child, you are not a man, you have no beard on your chin! How much longer are you going to fail in running your household properly? Don't you realize that your brother is commanding enormous armies? So you command your palace and household properly!" That is what Daddy wrote to me. Now how can I be a child and incapable of directing affairs when Daddy promoted me? How is it that, although I grew up with Daddy from when I was tiny, now some servant or other has succeeded in ousting me from Daddy's affections? So I am coming to Daddy right now, to have it out with Daddy about my unhappiness.

Yasmah-Addu probably was in over his head. His father sent him and his brother constant and detailed instructions, but Yasmah-Addu was not a competent ruler. We also have a letter to Yasmah-Addu from his older brother, scolding him for having lit the emergency flares that would call in troops from the region to rescue him in case of an invasion. Yasmah-Addu evidently lit them in response to a very minor raid that was immediately dealt with, and now, said his brother, the whole region will be rushing to your aid unnecessarily and Yasmah-Addu should send out letters *immediately* to say that everything is all right. It all sounds surprisingly modern—including the fact that someone could have a job for which he was unsuited because a powerful father backed him.

HAMMURABI'S EARLY YEARS AS KING

In short, when Hammurabi inherited the kingdom of Babylon he was a player, but not a terribly important one. All he could do was hold on to his territory, strengthen it, and be a good king. Being a good king meant living up to the well-defined ideals of kingship that had developed over the years by the old kings of Sumer and Akkad. It defined what he believed about his role and what he did.

Hammurabi and his people would have believed that the chief gods, Enlil and An, and the patron god of Babylon, named Marduk, had granted him the power to rule. The monument of Hammurabi's famous law collection and a wall painting of a king's investiture (the official act of making him king) in the palace of Mari show a king standing before a seated god. The king holds his hand in front of his mouth in a position of worship and respect, as a servant would stand in front of his master. (Anyone would have known what this gesture meant, as a modern person would recognize a military salute if he or she saw it in a picture.) The meaning of this image is clear: The king rules with the permission of the gods. It is the gods who give him power, but he is not himself a god. Rather, he is the gods' servant. One of his primary responsibilities is to maintain their "houses"—the temples—including the objects inside the temples. Statues of a king often show him carrying a basket on his head or carrying tools for building, symbolizing the work he must do for the gods. Gods were treated as important human guests might be. They were fed, through animal sacrifices and the cooking of ritual meals, housed, and given rich, elaborate furniture and gifts. And they were consulted, through the oracles, before important decisions were made.

Most importantly, the king was supposed to take care of his people, not as a god or as an owner, but as a loving shepherd. A shepherd guards his flock. He protects it, keeps order, and makes sure it is fed. He does not own it, but he is responsible for it. As intermediary to the gods, and as their servant, the king tried to ensure that the gods would provide "plenty." We do not know anything about Hammurabi's investiture, the ceremony that formally makes him king, as a coronation does a modern king or queen. It must have been much like that of Zimri-Lim's, for which there is a hymn that lists the royal insignia that the king is given—the crown, the throne, and the scepter of justice. The hymn mentions also that there is a mace bound to his body that symbolizes his right to control people (military force), and a mace that he grasps that signifies his symbolic power to "multiply the people." For ancient peoples, the highest blessing is that they have children and that their population increases. The hymn also says: "May he [the god] open for you the shining udder of heaven, and rain down for you the rains of heaven." These are literal rains, but because they come from an udder, they also stand for nourishment. The food that comes from an udder is the milk given to a baby. Milk made into butter or cheese was also a source of protein for the Mesopotamian people.

Many things could—and did—go wrong with crops, animals, and people, including floods or droughts, illnesses that seemed to come from nowhere (other illnesses could be recognized and dealt with), plagues of locusts, and invasions. There simply were a lot of things that were not in human control. The Mesopotamians understood that there were ways in which they were not masters of their fate. They trusted their king to intervene and help ensure that the gods would be kind to them.

THE SHEPHERD KING

Still, there was a great deal that the king could do to provide directly for his people by paying close attention to the things that *were* in human control. Maintaining the canals was essential to flood control and irrigation. The water from working canals meant life. If an ancient Babylonian was really angry with someone he might curse at them: "May your canal become clogged with sand!" The king (and his representatives) made sure that people got the water they needed and that no one upstream was diverting it. They punished people who did not take care of their canals or who carelessly flooded their neighbor's field. The king was involved in the collection of food, both to feed the gods and the people who depended on him—servants, soldiers, craftspeople making things for the palace or the temple. In fact, it is still unclear whether a craftsperson like a potter sold his work directly or whether he too was dependent on what the king gave him. The king collected, stored, and distributed food. Like a tribal sheik, or chief, keeping people fed was one of the leader's key responsibilities, and it was one that had gotten far more complicated as cities grew.

The shepherd/king was also responsible for the safety and security of his people. He alone had the power to organize and pay for the people and materials needed to build, maintain, and enlarge the city walls. These walls meant protection but were also signs of the king's power and prestige. Some were decorated. He raised troops as necessary from his own people, lending and borrowing troops to and from allied kings when necessary.

The king also had to protect his people through diplomacy. The king maintained good relations with neighboring kingdoms (when not attacking them) and tried to assure mutual pacts so that they would, in fact, lend troops and share information about what other kings were up to. The kings exchanged presents and sent letters by messengers. They also stationed "ambassadors" in one another's courts, though it is useful to know that the word we translate as "ambassador" also means "spy." They certainly functioned as both at the same time. The kings also arranged diplomatic marriages for their children at various times, trying to create and stabilize relations between city-states. Most of their diplomacy was carried out at a distance, through documents carried by messengers and representatives. The kings met one another only rarely.

THE KING AS JUDGE

The other important job of the king was to administer justice. We have seen that earlier kings also had law codes and displayed inscription about not letting the weak be oppressed by the powerful. (For modern people, the existence of slavery makes us doubt this, but the question of slavery in ancient times must be discussed later.) That did not mean that the king decided all disputes. He did render judgments on some cases (those involving murder for instance), and other cases could be appealed to him, but he was also responsible to see that local judges decided cases fairly. Witnesses would be called to testify and they would swear an oath before the gods to tell the truth. Relevant documents and other evidence would be examined.

In some ways this insistence on establishing justice is the most surprising part of the king's job. In other cultures and at other times, a leader is a warrior. His job is to prove his honor by smashing enemy heads. But Hammurabi does not emphasize that part of his job, and by his time, the kings of the region did not seem to ride into battle. Instead, in the words of the prologue to Hammurabi's laws, the king is empowered and entrusted by the gods to make sure justice "shines" all over the land, which is why the god of the sun is also the god of justice. Justice is a way of creating "law and order." It is a way of ordering and controlling people. The alternative is chaos, but the words suggest that people are entitled to protection and fairness from their king. The gods were not always fair, of course, but very few peoples believe that their god or gods are fair, according to human standards. The Mesopotamians had a poem called "The Lament of the Just Man." He, like the character Job in the Hebrew Bible, laments that he is just but tormented by the gods, while others are not punished by the gods for their wrongdoings. The king rules through law, not through violence.

The word *justice* meant something else too. The custom of a king's canceling personal debts in the first full year of his reign

At the top of the column inscribed with Hammurabi's code, a carving shows the sun god Shamash, also the god of justice, blessing the king with the right to administer law *(above)*. As Shamash sits on his throne, the king maintains a respectful pose, with his hand over his mouth, as the god passes him a scepter and a ring symbolizing the law.

was called "instituting justice." The rate of interest in ancient Mesopotamia was terribly high—20 to 33 percent even for a short loan, and a farmer or craftsman who had to borrow silver or grain might easily find himself unable to pay it back. In these instances, the lender could seize the borrower's property or force the man to sell himself or his wife and children into slavery for a period of three years. A new king would cancel personal loans (though not those between business partners, entered into in order to make a profit) and release people who had been sold into slavery to cover loans. Because many of the loans were created by the need to pay taxes, the king himself would be losing, but as author Marc Van De Mieroop says, he would demonstrate his power and mercy, and gain in goodwill and loyalty what he lost in revenue.

HAMMURABI AS KING

We have limited evidence of how Hammurabi carried out his duties in his first years as king. Still, we have inscriptions, letters (which, unfortunately, are not dated), and "year names." What we do know shows Hammurabi to have been a responsible ruler who carried out the traditional duties of a king. In his first year, he canceled personal debts. He was involved in the daily running of the kingdom—a "hands-on" administrator, not one who left everything to his officials. We have a letter in which he scolds an official that people have complained about. In another letter, Hammurabi checks up on an official by insisting that the man's livestock be counted, to make sure that he has not been stealing any animals while collecting livestock for the temple. He wrote very specific instructions telling the men of one town to dredge their irrigation canal and finish it within a month. Author Marc Van De Mieroop writes about Hammurabi reviewing a letter from a disgruntled farmer, written to an official. The farmer said, "I am not getting any water . . . for my sesame field. Don't tell me later 'You did not write to me.' . . . That sesame will die, and I have warned you."

Hammurabi also allocated land to make sure it was cultivated. He wanted people who were entitled to land to get it. He also wanted the share of sesame, wool, animals, and other products owed to the king to be delivered. The king owned much of the land and he would own even more later in his rule when he had conquered much of the region. People's lives depended, literally, on that land being productive. Some royal lands were rented out. Families farmed the land and sent part of their crops to the palace. Hammurabi had a lot of mouths to feed. These were not just his family and the palace servants and officials. He fed the gods (this food was also feeding some human beings, probably people of his family and the people who worked in the temple). Hammurabi fed (and sometimes clothed and gave gifts to) soldiers who had been recruited. Soldiers on campaigns received rations. Additionally, the many people working for the king—building city walls or canals, scribes, and craftspeople—were given beer (often barley beer), bread or grain, sesame oil, and wool to make clothes. (Cotton was not yet grown in the region and linen was not as common there as it was in Egypt.)

One of Hammurabi's main innovations as an administrator seems to have been to make many people less dependent on the palace than they had been. In exchange for doing their share of military duty (or, in times of peace, doing their share of work repairing city walls or canals), they would be given the right to farm certain fields rather than being given rations. This sounds as if they were going backward to a time when people had to provide their own food, as opposed to their being able to specialize in nonfarming occupations. In fact, some of the people to whom land was given would then rent out that land so that someone else farmed it and provided them with food. It made people less dependent on what the king gave them, and it gave them land that could be passed down to their children. This explains in part the tremendous amount of record keeping that went on in Babylon. All of these agreements about the land were written down on clay tablets, and the king and his officials always knew who owned the land, what rent or taxes was due to them, and if it had been paid.

KING HAMMURABI IN TIMES OF PEACE

For most of Hammurabi's reign, the year names refer to the creation or maintenance of canals and city walls, or to the building or restoration of temples. He also noted his contribution of major statues or other items to the temples, as in 1779 B.C., the fourteenth year of his reign, he "had made a throne finished with gold, silver, semi-precious stones and lapis-lazuli, like a blaze of light for [goddess] Inna of Babylon." His ninth year as king, 1784 B.C., "He dug the canal 'Hammurabi-means-abundance.'" Both the canal and the year name were reminders to the people that Hammurabi was fulfilling his duties to the people.

A few year names between the sixth and tenth years of Hammurabi's rule refer to battles. Year seven, 1786 B.C., was called "Hammurabi, the King, captured [the cities of] Uruk and Isin." This is the sort of instance when year names are not entirely useful, because we do not know what this means. There is no evidence that Hammurabi rules these cities after that year. The simplest evidence is the year names that a city used. Cities that Hammurabi ruled used his year names. Uruk and Isin did not. This early in his rule Hammurabi was still in no position to be challenging the kingdoms around him, so these "captures" may instead refer to minor raids, probably ones carried out at the instructions of a more powerful king.

Later in his reign, Hammurabi was in a position to fight and win, and he did. This was possible because the balance of power in the region shifted and he was able to take advantage of it.

CHAPTER

5

The Conquest of Larsa and Eshnunna

IN 1776 B.C., KING SHAMSHI-ADAD, RULER OF UPPER MESOPOTAMIA, DIED.
Yet again, the death of a powerful ruler and empire builder
resulted in the collapse of his empire. His elder son, Ishme-
Dagan, was able to maintain control of Ekallatum (the city
traditionally held by the family) but not the regions into which
Shamshi-Adad had expanded. The younger son, Yasmah-Addu,
the one his father accused of not knowing how to "take charge
of his house," may have been as incompetent as his father
feared. In any event, he immediately ceased to be the king of the
city he had ruled for his father, the ancient city of Mari, right
around the border between north and south Mesopotamia. His
older brother had promised that Yasmah-Addu would continue

to rule Mari "forever," but he was not strong enough to keep that promise.

The kingship of Mari was taken over by an outsider named Zimri-Lim. He was not of the city but was a tribesman from the Sim'alite tribes who came from northern Syria. However, on becoming king, he moved into Mari's huge and ancient palace and ruled like any other king. (Archaeologists have discovered the palace of Mari to have had about 300 rooms and walls as thick as 60 feet. It even had bathtubs!)

Shamshi-Adad's death destabilized the region. Mesopotamia had still been a collection of city-states, not a nation, but with the collapse of the northern Mesopotamian empire, more of the city-states were taken over again by the families that had once ruled them or by new kings. Author Amélie Kuhrt cites a letter sent by one of Zimri-Lim's officials that sums up the situation clearly. It said: "There is no king who is strong by himself: 10 or 15 kings follow Hammurabi of Babylon, as many follow Rim-Sin of Larsa, Ibalpiel of Eshnunna and Amutpiel of Qatna, while 20 kings follow Yarim-Lim of Yamkhad."

ELAM ATTACKS

Once "no king was strong by himself," the supreme ruler of Elam, Sukkalmah Siwe-palar-huppak, began to make a move. In 1767 B.C. he began to exchange presents with Zimri-Lim, Mari's new king. Both Elam and Mari had geographical and historical reasons to break with Eshnunna, and within a year or two, the king of Eshnunna was gone and his lands were ruled from Susa, in Elam.

Siwe-palar-huppak then began to act as if he was supreme ruler over Mari and Babylon. He told Hammurabi by letter: "Submit to my yoke, otherwise I will pillage your country." He ordered Hammurabi and Zimri-Lim to break off diplomatic relations with each other. They were to withdraw their representatives from each other's courts and stop exchanging gifts. He also demanded that Hammurabi send troops to help in Elam's invasion of Larsa, to the south, still ruled by King Rim-Sin. Hammurabi agreed, but his agreement was a ploy. He had discovered that Siwe-palar-huppak was also asking Rim-Sin for troops to use against Hammurabi. Hammurabi and Rim-Sin literally compared notes about this, exchanging the letters sent to them from Elam. As a result, neither sent troops to help Siwe-palar-huppak. He obviously had bad intentions toward them both.

Siwe-palar-huppak then invaded northern Mesopotamia, urging the kings of that area to join with him in a siege against Babylon. Hammurabi wrote to Zimri-Lim of Mari, and they swore a treaty to fight together against Siwe-palar-huppak. We have Hammurabi's letter in which he swears by the gods that he would "be at war with Siwe-palar-huppak" and would not receive servants or messengers from him and would never make peace with him without the approval of Zimri-Lim.

Zimri-Lim was king of Mari, but he also ruled various tribal lands. In particular, he remained close to his own people, the Sim'alite tribe, and so he was able to call in troops not only from his city and the lands surrounding it but from among the nomadic tribal peoples. According to author Marc Van De Mieroop, the nomads would have preferred not to be involved (they told Zimri-Lim's official this), but the official suggested to the king that he would "kill a criminal who is in prison and cut his head off, and parade it from village to village . . . so that the people become afraid and assemble soon." He said this would speed up the process of getting tribesmen to volunteer as soldiers.

Something worked—perhaps the official's threat, perhaps Zimri-Lim's old tribal connections—because Zimri-Lim was able to send thousands of city men and tribesmen to Hammurabi. Hammurabi responded, correctly, by having the tribesmen—hundreds at a time—eat his food in his presence.

He knew how to be an urban king, but he also knew how to be a tribal leader. Feeding troops, especially men from tribes, in the king's presence was a way of cementing a bond between them. By doing this, he proved himself responsible for them and they incurred a debt to him. By eating his food, they owed him their loyalty.

Troops from other regions also arrived. Zimri-Lim's father-in-law was the king of Yamkhad, far to the northwest, in what is now Syria. This is the land Zimri-Lim came from and it was his father-in-law of whom it was said, "Twenty kings follow Yarim-Lim of Yamkhad." Yarim-Lim made it clear that he was sending the troops for the sake of his son-in-law and that they were Zimri-Lim's troops, not Hammurabi's. Ishme-Dagan, the son of the late king Shamshi-Adad, now king of Ekallatum, also sent troops. The king recognized that Siwe-palar-huppak posed a threat to them all. Only King Rim-Sin of Larsa promised troops but did not send them.

MILITARY TACTICS

In a war like this, involving much of the region, many military tactics would have been used at the same time. Soldiers fought with bows and arrows and with battle-axes with bronze heads. They wore helmets of hardened leather—metal was still in very limited supply—and marched in rows with their shields overlapping to make a solid wall against enemy arrows. Different troops would have used different weapons. The unit of spearmen of course carried spears, but men who hunted for a living would probably have fought with nets and slingshots, the weapons they knew best. The highest technology was the "composite bow," made from layers of wood, horn, and sinew glued together. It would have shot an arrow farther and with greater accuracy than a bow made only of wood. The technology that was missing was the sword. Although men might carry knives to stab with, swords were not practical yet. Bronze was

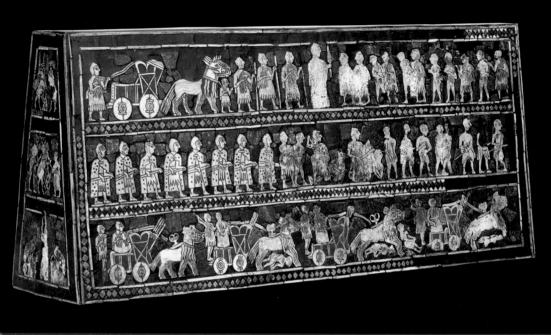

The emblem of Ur *(above)* consisted of two panels known as "War" and "Peace." The "War" panel of the standard, used as a rallying point in battle, displays images of chariots, each pulled by four donkeys, and cloaked warriors holding spears.

expensive and was not hard enough to hold its edge. It was iron that would later make swords possible.

The Sumerians had used war chariots made with solid (not spoked) wheels, drawn by donkeys. Horses had been introduced by Hammurabi's time, but seem not to have played much of a role in warfare. War chariots with two spoked wheels—lighter, faster, and easier to maneuver than the old four-wheeled ones— may or may not have been in use by this time.

For storming a city, nothing was more important than the "siege engine." Ramps of dirt would be built so that the siege engines could be pushed right against the city walls, allowing troops to get over walls. This did not always work: When the Elamites placed their siege engines around the walls of the city of Hiritium, a city on the border of Hammurabi's kingdom, the people of the city opened the irrigation canals and washed the ramps away. Ladders (to climb the walls) and battering rams were also used. The heavy metal tip of the battering ram would be wheeled, hard, against a gate or the city walls. Because the walls were brick, not stone, sometimes the invading soldiers could knock them down or make holes in them.

A siege itself could be a tactic, of course: If no people could enter or leave a city then the protecting walls became their prison. Eventually they would run out of food or become too weak to fight. Then they could easily be conquered or might simply surrender.

Hammurabi also raided Eshnunna, sending troops to burn crops and steal cattle in order to make the troops from that region worry about their homes.

People fighting wars nearly always hope that the war will not continue for too long, but the Mesopotamians had an additional reason for hoping this: Wars were fought seasonally at that time. The soldiers needed to be home in time to take care of their crops.

As in all battles, the deployment of troops and tactics required judgment, thought, and diplomacy. How best to use the forces available? What is the enemy likely to do and how can the soldiers be prepared? Earlier, Shamshi Adad had taught his sons in letters about these matters, including how to pick the best route for the soldiers to take. He recommended that they take the advice of more experienced war leaders. But in ancient Mesopotamia, decisions about battles, like all important decisions, also involved consulting the gods through the reading of omens. When a spy was able to warn the enemy and an attack involving 5,000 soldiers from Mari and Babylon failed, the Mari general sent some lambs to the expedition leader so that the omens could be consulted and a decision made when to continue the campaign.

THE FALL OF ELAM

Faced with the combined forces of much of the region, Elam was forced to retreat. The northern kings withdrew their support and their troops from Elam and offered allegiance to Hammurabi or Zimri-Lim. This seems partly their reckoning of who was likely to win and partly a return to older loyalties within the region. Elam was an outsider. When the Elamites looted the city of Eshnunna, the troops there deserted the sukkalmah's army. Their royal line had been destroyed, but a man named Silli-Sin, a military leader not of royal blood, became the new king. (Zimri-Lim suggested that Hammurabi pick the new king or declare himself king, but Hammurabi did not. We do not know if this was a mistake on his part or if Zimri-Lim was giving bad advice.)

The region fell into a new pattern of alliances after this war, but they were not stable ones. Although Siwe-palar-huppak said he wanted to make peace with Hammurabi, he made promises to Silli-Sin (in Eshnunna) and Rim-Sin (of Larsa) that he would support them against Hammurabi.

The year name that Hammurabi chose for 1764 B.C. was "with the help of the great gods, Hammurabi had defeated the armies of Elam from as far as Marhashi, of Subartu, Gutium, Eshnunna, and Malgium, which had arisen against him as a great mass, and he established the foundations of Sumer and Akkad." Author Marc Van De Mieroop says that is a claim to have defeated everyone east of the Tigris River, which was overstating the matter somewhat, but it is true that outside forces had risen up against Hammurabi. He had not started this war.

WAR WITH LARSA

Hammurabi had not begun the war with Elam. Whether he began the next one, which began almost immediately, depends on how we read the evidence.

Rim-Sin of Larsa was king of the largest region in southern Mesopotamia. In 1794 B.C., Rim-Sin had conquered the city-state of Isin, his old competition for control in the region. He was so proud of this that he named every year of the rest of his reign after it: "The first year after the sack of Isin," "The second year after the sack of Isin," and so on for the rest of his reign. With the conquest of Isin he controlled all the land up to the border of Hammurabi's Babylon.

When Siwe-palar-huppak of Elam had asked both Hammurabi and Rim-Sin for troops to fight each other, Rim-Sin had written that his troops stood ready to help Hammurabi if Elam attacked, but he never sent the troops. If Elam had conquered all the rest of Mesopotamia, he would not have been safe either, but instead of helping he seems to have decided to wait and see what happened.

Who started the war between Babylon and Larsa? A representative of Mari in Babylon said that Larsa did: "He [Rim-Sin] is hostile to Hammurabi. Military squadrons of his continuously enter Hammurabi's country to pillage and steal." Diplomatic relations between the two regions had broken off, said the man from Mari. In his declaration of war, Hammurabi also said that Rim-Sin had pillaged his country, but it seems clear that he was also angry over Rim-Sin's failure to support him during the war with Elam. Hammurabi said that he had sought through oracles the approval of the gods Shamash (god of justice) and Marduk (patron god of Babylon) and that they gave their approval for the attack.

The kingdom of Larsa (named for its main city, although the region was also called Yambutbal) was not well defended. Rim-Sin was an old man by this time, which may or may not have affected his ability to lead. The representative of Mari told his king, that Rim-Sin's soldiers were worried. They wondered "where will the enemy engage us?" The man from Mari said the country was afraid and ready to rebel. This suggests that Rim-Sin was failing in his role of shepherd-king. His people did not feel safe, and they did not remain loyal.

Most of the country was conquered easily. Mashkan-shapir (where the king's brother was staying) and the old cities of

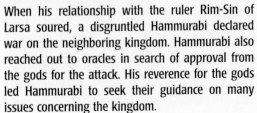

When his relationship with the ruler Rim-Sin of Larsa soured, a disgruntled Hammurabi declared war on the neighboring kingdom. Hammurabi also reached out to oracles in search of approval from the gods for the attack. His reverence for the gods led Hammurabi to seek their guidance on many issues concerning the kingdom.

Nippur and Isin fell at once. The city of Larsa itself, with Rim-Sin in command, held out during a six-month siege. Even though allies helped Hammurabi, they could not breach Larsa's walls, and the siege continued until the people of the city were eating straw and chaff. Although Rim-Sin escaped, Hammurabi's soldiers were later able to capture him. (We do not know what happened next to Rim-Sin.)

HAMMURABI'S NEW LANDS

Hammurabi's behavior after his victory in Larsa was typical of how he dealt with conquered lands, if the people of that land promised him their loyalty. Although he destroyed the city's walls, he did not destroy or pillage the city. Instead, he set out to establish himself as the legitimate king of the land and to restore order and good rule. He dealt with raiding tribesmen—major disruptions in a Mesopotamian city were often followed by raiding tribesmen. Then he named the year—in Larsa and the surrounding lands—"The year that Hammurabi became king," using the formula that a king used when he inherited a throne. In Babylon it was "The year that Hammurabi with the help of the gods An and Enlil, went before the army and by the supreme power which the great gods had given him conquered the land Yamutbal and its king, Rim-Sin." But after that, the regions would share year names, and Hammurabi tended to that region as he did the one he had inherited from his father. There is no evidence of his punishing the people, raiding the land for slaves (although this certainly happened after wars), pillaging its temples, or any of the other behaviors we might associate with the behaviors of a king toward the people he has conquered. Rather, he exercised his kingship as a good shepherd and as the servant of the gods of those cities, constructing temples there and caring for and improving its canals. Additionally, he canceled the personal debts of the people there as he had his first year as king of Babylon. He put an official, a

Babylonian man named Sin-iddinam, in charge of the region. He did what was necessary to keep these lands functioning normally: The land had to be irrigated, protected from floods, and farmed. Otherwise, people would begin to starve. That would be bad kingship, and a starving people would not be likely to remain loyal to their new king.

In conquering the lands held by Rim-Sin, Hammurabi had made himself the most important king in Mesopotamia, king of the largest region. It was not a country exactly, as we would now use the term, but it was a centralized state under his control, with his representatives in place there and the people paying tribute to him. He was responsible for them and to their gods.

6

The Fall of Eshnunna and Mari

IT CAN BE DIFFICULT TO FOLLOW THE HISTORY OF WARFARE AND ALLIANCES among the Mesopotamian city-states. Threatened by a common enemy, two kings from nearby city-states might agree to help each other with troops or with information from their spies. Yet having achieved a victory or suffered a loss, each might seek to make alliances with opposite sides. Kings and local leaders of the smaller city-states "followed" the king of a large one, but they might change allegiances so as to ally themselves with whoever seemed to be winning a war. During a time of upheaval—a big war, the death of a powerful king—they might reassert their control over their own city.

As there were dozens of city-states, in a period of instability it can be impossible to keep track of who was doing what and why. Even when we have letters between kings, the letters are not dated. Also, the kings were often engaged in many military operations at the same time. For example, during the time that King Zimri-Lim of Mari sent troops to Hammurabi during the wars with Elam and Larsa, he was having trouble keeping order in his own northern territory. Local kings were trying to reclaim the independence of their cities; tribal peoples were going on raids. "Put polite pressure on Hammurabi" to release some of the troops, Zimri-Lim instructed one of his generals after nearly two years of conflicts. Hammurabi told the general, "Be quiet!" He said he needed five or ten days to see what the king of Eshnunna would do. Zimri-Lim did not get his troops back.

THE WAR WITH ESHNUNNA

Eshnunna was politically important in part because of its location. Trade routes ran through it, so it was to Hammurabi's advantage to make peace with Eshnunna's new king, the ex-military commander Silli-Sin. The two set about negotiating a treaty, and because we have letters and records of their negotiations, we can see how such matters were handled.

In this instance, the new king sent an "envoy" to Hammurabi. Hammurabi released the Eshnunnan prisoners that he held. Hammurabi sent a "small tablet"—a draft of the treaty—to Silli-Sin. If each king agreed to the terms (which unfortunately we do not know) then each would swear to a copy of a large tablet, the treaty itself. But Hammurabi was unable to conclude a treaty with Silli-Sin, and so he tried to create an alliance in a different way. Although we have no details of the arrangement, Silli-Sin would name the year 1764 B.C., "The year that Silli-Sin married the daughter of Hammurabi." Still, the alliance would not hold.

In 1762 B.C., King Zimri-Lim of Mari also allied himself with Silli-Sin through an exchange of expensive gifts: gold, silver, and other presents, including a gold vase. Zimri-Lim submitted himself to Eshnunna's rule. He was not surrendering—he would still remain king of Mari—but he would follow Eshnunna. Hammurabi was furious, seeing this alliance as a threat to Babylon. "It would be unlikely if in two months I did not take revenge on him and make him kneel in the dust!" he said.

Hammurabi attacked Eshnunna first. We have no record of whether this endangered his daughter or if he was able to get her out of the city safely. Although he overcame Eshnunna, he does not seem to have fully taken over these lands as he had in the south, in Larsa. He did not take over the main palace but instead took over or built a different one. The actions that tell us that a land has a new king are missing here: He does not cancel personal debts and the Eshnunnan region does not begin to use the same year names as the Babylonian Empire. In any event, his control over the region was incomplete and insecure. About six years later, in 1756 B.C., Hammurabi's army again attacked Eshnunna, which had probably tried to reassert its independence. His year name says, "He destroyed Eshnunna with a great flood." Historians such as Marc Van De Mieroop suggest that Hammurabi may have changed the course of rivers and canals temporarily and in that way brought down the city walls and flooded the city, something that was done at other times in the region.

Even before Hammurabi flooded Eshnunna, power in northern Mesopotamia was so fragmented that Hammurabi was able to march his troops through it without trouble. The north had never regained its unity after the death of Shamshi-Adad in 1776 B.C. Zimri-Lim, whose kingdom of Mari lay on the edge of Shamshi-Adad's region, had controlled part of it. Shamshi-Adad's older son, Ishme-Dagan was able to retain control of the city of Ekallatum, the family's "dynastic seat." His younger brother, the oft-scolded Yasmah-Addu, was expelled by (or perhaps killed by) the people of Mari as soon as his powerful father died: It was then that Zimri-Lim took the throne there. Even Ishme-Dagan's control of his city may have been insecure.

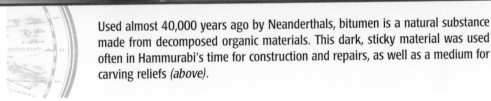

Used almost 40,000 years ago by Neanderthals, bitumen is a natural substance made from decomposed organic materials. This dark, sticky material was used often in Hammurabi's time for construction and repairs, as well as a medium for carving reliefs (above).

He had supplied troops for Hammurabi's defeat of Elam, but when he asked Hammurabi for troops, his messengers asked in the most humble terms possible: "Our Lord [Ishme-Dagan] is like a doormat under your feet," they said. (This would not have sounded as dramatically wimpy at the time as it does now. As the language used to describe an ideal king is—to modern ears—very boastful and exaggerated, the language of polite humility was also extreme.) But Ishme-Dagan was not really feeling humble. Hammurabi's messenger said that Ishme-Dagan had complained that Hammurabi treated him with less respect than he did Zimri-Lim. Hammurabi wrote to Ishme-Dagan as a father—a superior—but to Zimri-Lim as a brother—an equal. Hammurabi refused to send soldiers to Ishme-Dagan.

THE INVASION OF MARI

Ishme-Dagan should not have envied the king of Mari's relationship with Hammurabi. In 1761 B.C., Hammurabi turned on his old ally, whom he had not forgiven for siding with Eshnunna. Because the best archive we have for this period is the one in Mari, and Hammurabi would eventually destroy the palace after first removing much of his own correspondence with Zimri-Lim, we know less about the region after Hammurabi conquered that city.

This is how it happened.

Marc Van De Mieroop shows how, back when the sukkalmah of Elam was the leader the kings called "father," he made a decision that sowed seeds of discord between Hammurabi and Zimri-Lim. The disagreement—over who would rule a city on the Euphrates called Hit—demonstrates a great deal about how disputes were settled as well as what was at stake for the two kings when they claimed a city.

The dispute arose because Hit was between Mari and Babylon and each had a particular reason for wanting to rule it. Hammurabi wanted Hit because it was a good source of bitumen. Bitumen is a black tar, or pitch, that wells up from the ground in pools. It was used as mortar in that region, as we use cement to hold bricks together today. Hardened into solid chunks, bitumen could be carved like stone. But Hammurabi wanted it for its other use: as caulk to waterproof and seal the boats he used for trade and as transportation. "Your country's power lies in donkeys and chariots," he had his scribes write to Zimri-Lim, but "my country's power lies in ships."

Hit's importance to Mari was not as a source of bitumen. Instead, it had legal importance. A part of the Euphrates River that flowed there was used for the "river ordeal." This was an old way of testing the claims of two parties in a legal case when more ordinary methods failed. If documents could be produced to prove (for instance) who had the rights to a disputed piece of land or witnesses could swear an oath and testify that they had seen someone commit a crime, then the case could be decided on this ordinary testimony. In other cases, witnesses could not agree or there was no proof of the crime; for instance, in a case concerning an accusation of sorcery or one in which a woman was accused of adultery but had not actually been caught in bed with a man who was not her husband. Or, sometimes, people both claimed a piece of land and the records were missing. In these instances, the person accused or the people in disagreement would be ordered to submit to the "river ordeal." In a special part of the river, they would have to swim a certain distance, sometimes underwater. In this way, they were submitting themselves to the judgment of the god of the river. If they survived, then they were innocent or the oath they had taken was considered true. At other times, people would refuse the ordeal, giving up their claims. The practice dates from before Hammurabi but survived through medieval times and was revived during the witchcraft trials of colonial America, except that in those American trials, the accused proved her innocence by drowning while the guilty person survived to be rescued and then executed.

The negotiations over the rule of Hit were long and complex. Hammurabi even suggested co-ruling it. Much of the negotiations sound like modern diplomacy. The kings discussed the rule of other disputed cities, asserted the lasting friendship between their cities, and repeated that, of course, they each had the other's best interests at heart. They said, truly,

When Hammurabi attacked Mari, he also destroyed the royal palace of Zimri-Lim, Mari's king. Hammurabi's soldiers knocked down walls, which inadvertently preserved the objects inside for later discovery in the 1930s. Cuneiform tablets detailing political affairs, cylinder seals, and wall paintings survived the siege, and some of the ancient structures continue to stand in Syria (above).

that they needed to remain military allies. But Zimri-Lim also had an expert examine the entrails or liver of two lambs, asking the gods, "Should Zimri-Lim give up Hit to Hammurabi?" The diviner said no.

Zimri-Lim and Hammurabi fought together against Larsa and then against Elam, but without resolving the question of Hit. The sukkalmah had in fact ruled that Hit belonged to Mari, but Hammurabi continued to dispute this. He was less than willing to provide troops to Zimri-Lim—or even to return Zimri-Lim's troops when he needed them. So, when Hammurabi discovered that Zimri-Lim had promised allegiance to Silli-Sin of Eshnunna, Hammurabi was angry, but he may also have been using it as an excuse. He said, "Since he [Zimri-Lim] has seized the hem of the robe of Eshnunna's leader, I want to make him pay for it!"

Hammurabi did. Mari fell within four months of Hammurabi's defeat of Eshnunna. This time, his troops looted the ancient palace. In Hammurabi's year name for 1760 B.C., he summed up his victories and achievements. He said he "dug the canal called 'Hammurabi-means-abundance-for-the-people'" and "provided water of abundance for Nippur, Eridu, Ur, Larsa, Uruk, and Isin." (These are the cities in the south that became fully integrated into his kingdom with the fall of Larsa.) Also he "restored Sumer and Akkad which had been scattered; overthrew in battle the army of Mari and Malgium; subjugated Mari and its villages and the many cities of the mountain land of Subartu, Ekallatum, all of Burunda and the land of Burunda and the land of Zamaqum on the back of the Tigris up to the Euphrates and caused them to dwell at his command and in friendship."

In using the phrase *Sumer and Akkad*, the traditional south and north of Mesopotamia, and in listing all those cities, he is saying that he has conquered all of Mesopotamia. The year name was something of an exaggeration, as year names often were. In the future, he would continue to name years for the defeat or slaughter of enemies in the Subartu Mountains. Evidently they did not entirely "dwell at his command," but continued to rebel. He would also return in two years to sack Mari, destroying its walls and turning it into a land of ruin and desolation. People fled, were captured and deported, or killed. Some eventually settled in small villages in the area, but the great city of Mari ceased to exist. (Ironically, Hammurabi did archaeologists and historians a favor: It was the destruction of Mari that collapsed the city, preserving it until it was excavated in the 1930s.)

Still, even if the year name was an exaggeration, it does show the size of the kingdom Hammurabi now controlled—the biggest region since Sargon the Great. His claim that he caused the region to dwell "in friendship," like his claim on the stela of his laws that he has caused the region to dwell "in peace," may sound strange to us. It sounds a little like a modern general's claim to have "pacified" a region, which is a polite way of saying that he has beaten the people so thoroughly that they cannot fight anymore. That may be an accurate description of what Hammurabi did—or tried to do—in some regions. He destroyed Mari, though not all its people. In others areas, like the south, he truly seems to have tried to create a peaceful, unified, and prosperous region.

CHAPTER

7

The Laws of Hammurabi

ALTHOUGH HISTORIANS SUCH AS MARC VAN DE MIEROOP HAVE LABORI- ously reconstructed the story of Hammurabi's battles, much of what we know about Hammurabi—and his times—comes from the law collection, excavated between 1901 and 1902. From the time it was first translated, it has been called The Code of Hammurabi. But what is this "code?"

A BLACK STONE STELA

It is useful to begin again with the code as an object: a seven and a half foot tall, slightly cone-shaped black stone column called a stela. Although it can now be found in the Louvre Museum in Paris, archaeologists found it in Susa, in Elam, where it had been taken by invaders as war loot. Originally, it stood in the courtyard of a temple to the god Shamash, king of justice and also of the sun, in the city of Sippar. Sippar was part of the lands Hammurabi had inherited from his father. It is also the city that called Shamash its patron god. So the original law collection was not meant to be in an archive where only scholars could see it. It was meant to be seen by everyone, even though most people could not read.

The first thing most people would have noticed about the stela was that picture on the top third of its front. Ordinary people would have understood what this picture meant. They would have recognized the god. He sits with his feet on mountains, wearing the three-horned crown of a god. Rays of sunlight extend out from his shoulders, showing which god he is and that justice is meant to shine all over the land, just as the sun does. For a Babylonian, especially one of that region, recognizing Shamash would have been as easy as it is for a Christian to recognize Mary as the young woman with a halo and a baby in her arms.

Shamash hands Hammurabi a rod and coiled rope (some say it is a ring). These are the insignia, the signs, of kingship. They appear also in other pictures. They were the recognized symbols that showed that the king had received the proper authority from the gods to rule and to administer justice in the land. The king holds his hand in front of his mouth in a position of respect and reverence. That was the proper way for a king to stand before a god, as it was the proper way for a man to stand before the king, as shown in other pictures and statues.

We do not know if this is an actual portrait of the king. There are other statues from the same time that are not of the king but which show someone who looks just like that. Although we would like to know what Hammurabi looked like, it would not have been important at the time whether it was a portrait of him or not. He had ruled many years by the time the stela was carved and installed in a courtyard—so many years that in those days

Carvings and reliefs depicting the Babylonian sun god Shamash were common, as he was one of the most popular gods in the kingdom. All who appeared before Shamash, who was also the god of justice, are seen standing with their hands over their mouths in a gesture of respect and deference *(above)*.

he would have been the only king that many people had known. Also, the stela was set up next to another statue, called Hammurabi, King of Justice. (His year name for 1771 B.C. says so.)

So that picture means that ordinary people would have known that Shamash, god of justice, had given Hammurabi the right to rule and to dispense justice. Whether it means Shamash actually gave him these laws—as, in the Bible, God gives the laws to Moses, is less clear. Hammurabi does not say so; nor do earlier kings who made law collections.

THE TEXT OF THE CODE OF HAMMURABI

Of course the code is also the words that are carved below the picture and on the other side of the stela. There is one blank area where the Elamite king Shutruk-Nahhunte erased some of the words when he looted the stela (and many others) in the twelfth century B.C. The conquering king erased parts of the other monument he took and had his own inscriptions put there, but the blank area on this stela was never filled.

The words on the stela are inscribed very carefully. Cuneiform had developed so that it could be written quickly on soft clay. Carving it into hard rock was much more difficult. The style of the inscriptions—the script itself—was old-fashioned by Hammurabi's time. He does not pretend that the stela is older than it is, but that style gives it more dignity. When letters are carved into the stone on a modern court building or government office, an old style of lettering is chosen. Using an older style ties it to the past and gives it authority, and Hammurabi meant his law monument to have a great deal of authority, even after he was dead. He says so.

There are three parts to the text carved on the stela. There are the laws themselves—between 275 and 300 of them, including some of the ones that were erased but have been rediscovered from copies of the laws that scribes made before the stela was stolen. Before the laws comes a prologue and after the laws comes an epilogue. These sound more like poetry than like the dry language of the laws listed.

THE CLAIMS OF A JUST KING

In the prologue, Hammurabi explains how the chief gods, An and Enlil, gave him the kingship. He lists the cities he rules and their gods and temples. He explains how he cares for the gods and temples of the cities he conquered. From the point of view of people of Hammurabi's time, he is showing that he has a right to rule those cities. So, the prologue repeats—in words—what the picture shows but makes it more specific by naming the cities the gods have given to him. Also, Hammurabi says that the gods gave supreme power to Marduk, the patron god of Babylon, which makes it the most important city in the region.

From a modern point of view, Hammurabi is doing something else too: He is helping us to date the stela. We know that Hammurabi did not control all those cities until almost the end of his reign, so the law stela could not have been written until then. Putting it up was not the act of a new king, explaining how he hoped to rule, but of an old and victorious one, asserting his intention and his power to rule justly.

The epilogue is about justice and kingship. Hammurabi says that he is the king of justice. He takes care of his people and protects them, even poor people, children, and widows, from oppression by the powerful. Let anyone who feels wronged, he says, come and have the stela read out to him and be comforted. Hammurabi unites people, he says. M.E.J. Richardson's translation shows that some of his words are gentle. "I have set the people of the land of Sumer and Akkad securely on my knees. They have prospered under my protection. I have made the people lie down in well-watered pastures. I am the shepherd who brings peace." The language is nearly the language of a biblical hymn, except that here it is the king—not a god—who is the shepherd. The history of the place reminds us how important is this image of offering "well-watered pastures." We cannot ever forget that water meant prosperity. Water meant life.

Hammurabi addresses kings who will rule after him, as well as speaking to the people of his time. Marc Van De Mieroop writes that Hammurabi says of any future king, "May he guide his people correctly. May he judge their cases and give decisions. May he remove the evil and the wicked from his land. May he make his people happy." Hammurabi means, that future kings should follow *his* laws, and he calls down terrible curses on any king who changes his laws or does not respect them. The gods will curse that king. He will have no children.

THE LAWS OF HAMMURABI

The laws cover a wide range of subjects. Some are what we would call criminal law: what should happen to people who steal or kill. Others concern matters as varied as marriage and divorce, what should happen to a farmer who floods his neighbor's field, and how much someone must pay to have a boat built.

The form of the laws is all the same. Rather than saying that stealing is illegal or "Thou shalt not" kill or lie, the laws say what happens if someone does these things. They all start with the word *if*. "If" a certain thing happens: *If* a man marries a woman, but she cannot bear him any children, *if* a barber cuts off the distinctive lock of hair that identifies a slave, *if* a builder is careless in his work and the house he builds collapses and kills the man who owns it. The second part of each law says what should happen: The man whose wife cannot bear him children may marry again but must care for his first wife. The barber shall have his hand cut off. The builder whose carelessness has caused someone to die shall himself be put to death. (If the house collapses and kills the owner's son, then the builder's son is put to death instead.)

"AN EYE FOR AN EYE"

It is examples like this last one that were of particular interest when the laws were discovered and translated in 1902. It is the principle of "an eye for an eye, a tooth for a tooth" that appears in the laws of the Hebrew Bible and until the discovery of Hammurabi's code, the Hebrews were given credit for having come up with the idea. Modern laws in Western countries do not say that a man who cuts off someone else's arm will have

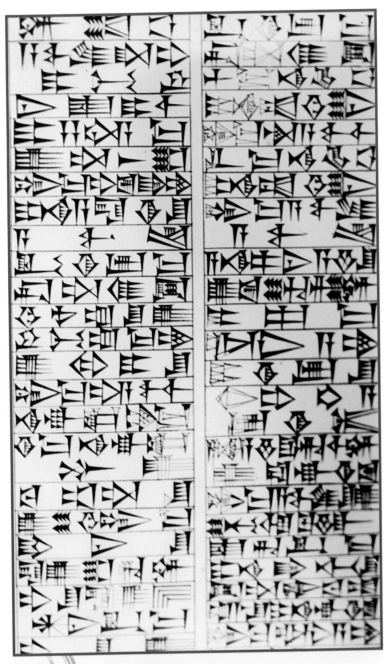

The Code of Hammurabi *(above)* is one of the most fully developed ancient legal systems in existence. Consisting of almost 300 laws, the code was extensive in listing laws concerning family, criminal, or civil affairs.

the same done to him. He is more likely to go to jail. Still, most ordinary people continue to cite this principle as fair. People who believe in the death penalty, for instance, still say "an eye for an eye, a tooth for a tooth, a life for a life." Although the Christian Bible suggested another standard of justice—that those who are injured should "turn the other cheek" and forgive their enemies, "an eye for an eye" still seems fair—as a general principle—to most people. And, as far as we know, Hammurabi said it first.

We do not know how Hammurabi came up with this idea. Although we now know that he inherited and was influenced by a number of earlier law collections and borrowed freely from them, these earlier laws all specify monetary payments in the case of physical injuries to another person. Someone who injured someone else paid them.

WHAT THE LAWS SAY

Although the establishment of the "eye for an eye" principle was Hammurabi's biggest legal innovation, his law collection remains the most important for other reasons, even after archaeologists discovered earlier ones. Partly that's because it is the longest and covers the most subjects. It certainly does not have a law and penalty for everything, but it does cover many legal and social issues that could arise. (Also it is still the longest unbroken Babylonian text we have. Clay tablets are small and unless they have been fired in a kiln or burned when their storage place was destroyed, they are fragile.) Although the laws are not separated into categories on the stela, it is possible to see that there is a rough grouping of laws on the same subject.

Things to do with legal cases: such as someone accused of swearing a false oath or judges changing their verdict after a case is decided.

Laws about property: stealing, slaves who run away or are stolen, kidnapping, breaking into someone's house. If someone loots a house while helping put out a fire in it, he shall be cast into that same fire.

Laws about the land that involve men who are doing military service or are otherwise working for the king: The land given to a man for military service or to a woman who had been given to the temple as a priestess was carefully protected.

Other laws about the land: If a man rents out a field but does not plant it, he owes the field's owner the amount of grain he should have raised. If a man does not care for the banks of his irrigation canals and it floods a neighbor's field, he owes the field's owner the amount of grain that has been destroyed.

Financial matters, including things that have to do with merchants and loans: (The missing parts of the stela are in this part.) If a man is robbed while transporting goods for someone as part of a business arrangement he must swear before a god that he really was robbed but he is not held financially responsible for the loss.

The family, including marriage, adultery, divorce, adoption, incest, inheritance, property rights of women including priestesses and divorced women: If a man adopts a child and teaches the child his craft, the parents cannot reclaim the child. If a man has left property to his wife, his children cannot try to take it back after his death.

Assault: If a child shall strike his father, they shall cut off his hand.

Rates of payment for professional services (doctors, boat builders, house builders) and penalties for these professionals if someone is injured as a result of their work: No suing a doctor who injures a patient during surgery—just cut off his hand.

Agriculture: everything from how much it costs to rent an ox or goat to what happens if an ox gores someone to who is responsible if something happens to rented animals or animals that are in a shepherd's care.

Rates: of hire for animals, boats, and wagons; of pay for various kinds of craftsmen and laborers.

Ownership and sale of slaves: If a man buys a slave and within a month the slave turns out to have epilepsy, the man can return the slave and get back what he paid for the slave.

A LAW "CODE?"

Hammurabi's law code is so famous that most people are surprised to find out that it is not a law code at all. The French general Napoléon who declared himself emperor of Europe in the early 1800s created a real "law code." His code covered every case and ensured that everyone he ruled would live under the same laws. Hammurabi's code does not cover everything. (For

Slaves

There were three classes of people in Babylon, but the only one we fully understand is *wardum*—slaves. Slaves belong to someone else, not to themselves. Slaves who tried to escape and anyone who helped them were punished.

Still, we make a mistake if we apply to Babylon's enslaved people and the people who owned them all the judgments we hold in the twenty-first century, after the enslavement of Africans and all of what that has meant for American and world history. Ancient peoples—Egyptians, Mesopotamians, Greeks, Romans, and Hebrews—had slaves and we are bad historians if we do not try to understand what that meant at the time.

The first slaves in Mesopotamia, long before Hammurabi, were people captured during raids in the mountains. The ideogram (picture sign) for a slave was the sign for a man or woman plus the sign for mountain. Originally, slaves worked for the king as soldiers or building roads, canals, or walls. By Hammurabi's time, some slaves worked in private instance, it does not impose a penalty for ordinary murder. It does not say what should happen if a collapsing house kills the owner's son, but the builder does not have a son.) Also there was no way for Hammurabi to have imposed these laws. Most law cases were decided locally, by local judges, and there is no evidence that they referred to a body of law to make their rulings. So, a better description than law code would be "law collection."

Most surprising is that these were not laws at all. In fact, there was no word for *law*. Author Martha T. Roth states that Hammurabi says after listing them that "these are the just decisions that Hammurabi the able king has established, and thereby has

houses. Captured people might become slaves—or they might be given land or workshops of their own. Some male and female slaves were scribes, which means they were highly educated.

A high-class man who got into debt might have to sell himself and his family into a three-year period of slavery. Other slaves were bought and sold and would not be freed after three years. Still, a slave could marry a free person and their children would be free. They could conduct business, own or borrow money, and sometimes buy their own freedom. So a free person could be enslaved and an enslaved person could become free. Slaves were identified by a special haircut—a mark that would go away by itself, unlike a scar. Additionally, slavery was not based on ethnicity or race. As the Sumerians, Akkadians, Amorites, and other peoples took power, they did not enslave the people they knocked out of power.

As modern people, we cannot easily understand how a "just" king would allow slavery, but we can try to recognize that slavery did not mean all the things then that it does to us today.

directed the land along the course of truth and the correct way of life." This suggests that they were his rulings on particular cases. It is possible that some of them were that, although some of them were also inherited from previous kings. But there is no evidence that they were applied to real cases. Archaeologists have discovered many records of law cases, but only one refers to the decision on the stela. When records tell us of the rates of pay for different jobs, they do not match the ones on the stela. When we have a record of a case concerning something that is listed on the stela (a temple priestess and her control of land she has inherited), but the case is decided without referring to the stela. Sometimes we can see that decisions have been made that follow the principles set out on the stela. One letter says that a slave shall be put to death because he killed a child. But other documents refer to prison sentences and there is no mention of prison sentences on the stela at all. This seems confusing, and historians find it confusing too.

Additionally, these laws may seem harsh—the death penalty is used for a wide range of crimes and "an eye for an eye" is harsher than the fines paid for such crimes in earlier law codes. There are two things that can be said about that. The first is that while cutting off the hand of a child who hits his father seems harsh, later law codes, like the one in the Bible, say that the child who hits a parent shall be put to death. The other is that there is little evidence that some of the harsher punishments were carried out.

What the laws on the stela do show is what Hammurabi meant by "justice" and what we might also call fairness.

WHAT DID HAMMURABI THINK WAS "JUST?"

Aside from "an eye for an eye," some other general principles are evident in the laws. One of these also tells us that there were three classes of people in Babylon at that time. The penalties were different for harming each of the three classes and each paid a different amount for such things as medical care. We

While the consequences of breaking Hammurabi's code seemed harsh, it appears as if the verdicts of law cases were not based on inscriptions of the stela. Tablets recording legal proceedings in cuneiform *(above)* found by archaeologists often contain information that conflicts with Hammurabi's code.

do not have good translations for any of the three classes, except the one that means "slave." The word for the highest class (*awilu*) is the word that sometimes just means a man or a woman. In the laws, it often means the people who not only pay the most for medical services but also the only people who are avenged by the "eye for an eye" rule. If a person of this class blinds another, his eye shall be put out. If he blinds the eye of an ordinary person, then he pays that person a fine. (The "ordinary person" category seems to refer to people who are palace or temple dependents, rather than people who own their own property. It's not clear which class a highly skilled artisan would be.) If a person of that highest class blinds the eye of a slave, he pays half the slave's value and he pays it to the slave's owner, not to the person he hurt.

The other principle of the laws has to do with responsibility. If a man rents a donkey and a lion kills it, it is not his fault and it is the owner's loss. But if the man causes the donkey's death by abuse or neglect, then he has to replace it. If someone rents a field and plants it and everything is destroyed by a storm, then that is what even modern insurance companies call "an act of god" and it's not his responsibility. He does not owe anything to the person whose field he rented. The laws will not make people suffer hardship if they have done what they are supposed to have done. If a woman's husband runs away or is away at war and she moves in with another man, the law will punish her if she has been provided for but not if she is going hungry.

So when Hammurabi claims that he has established justice in the land, he does not mean that he has established a system of laws or of abstract principles like "people shall be punished only for things that are their fault." Hammurabi actually lived so long ago that people did not yet have a way of talking about abstract principles. They had to use examples, and Hammurabi's stela gives enough examples to make it clear what he thinks a just world looks like, what its rules are. What the stela says is that in an orderly and just society, people should not lie under oath or steal things, even from widows who cannot defend themselves. A military officer cannot take advantage of the men he is in charge of. (Hammurabi says that he protects the weak from being oppressed by the powerful.) A husband and wife have responsibilities to each other, even if the wife cannot bear children or if she gets a terrible disease. The rate of pay for different jobs should be reasonable and fair. If people injure or kill someone or destroy property through carelessness or evil intent, then they pay a penalty, but if something happens that they could not have foreseen or prevented, then they will not be punished.

IDEALS VERSUS REALITY

Some of what Hammurabi considered just, we would not. He protects some but not all rights of women. He allows slavery. He lists different punishments, depending on the social class of the person injured. For these differences of belief, we must remember that Hammurabi lived a long time ago and in a different culture. We might remember that women had more rights in ancient Babylonia than they did 1,000 years later in that region—and more than they had in the late nineteenth century in America and England, when a married woman could not own property or sign a legal document.

And we might remember that the Egyptian pharaohs had no such concept as "justice." Egyptian law said that what is pleasing to pharaoh is just and what pharaoh dislikes is evil. End of discussion. The Mesopotamian kings were struggling toward an important and valuable ideal: They were responsible for creating a just and orderly society, one in which evil people are removed and the others are safe and prosperous. Hammurabi says this particularly clearly.

Of course that does not mean that justice always prevailed, and Hammurabi knew that. At the end of the epilogue to the stela he not only tells future kings to follow his model but he addresses someone he calls "the wronged man." The wronged man is supposed to come to the stela and have it read out to him and be comforted. This might suggest someone consulting the stela to see how his or her law case should be decided or that the person should go straight to Hammurabi for a just decision. But because the stela is not a law book, and it was meant to outlive him, there is another way of understanding these words. If a decision was unjust, or if a later king does not follow Hammurabi's model, or if the region is in turmoil, then the person should come and listen to the words on the stela—not just the "laws," but the words about peace and justice and order. The person should be comforted by this possibility—this ideal—and should bless Hammurabi for putting it into words. In other words, the stela is both an ideal and an expression of how Hammurabi wanted to be remembered.

8

The Babylonian Empire and Hammurabi's Legacy

IN HAMMURABI'S LAST FOUR OR FIVE YEARS AS KING, HE ERECTED THE monument with his law collection inscribed on it and set about ruling the lands he now controlled. It did not end the battles— the year 1754 B.C. was called the year Hammurabi "slaughtered all of the enemies of the Subartu Mountains"—but most year names refer to building or raising walls. The last year he named, 1750 B.C., was "Hammurabi, the King, put up the wall of Sippar, the eternal city of Utu, with a large amount of earth and raised it up like a mountain." As with much of the language of the time, the exaggerated description of the height of the wall was a standard one that many kings had used. We cannot even be sure Hammurabi had ever seen a mountain.

Because Hammurabi is best known for his law code—and was best remembered for it by the kings who came after him—we and they know him best as a man of peace who brought justice and order to the lands. A lesser-known stela, cited by author Marc Van De Mieroop, says he is a "mighty warrior, exterminator of enemies . . . destroyer of enemy lands, who puts an end to wars, who resolves disputes, who destroys soldiers like figurines of clay." Obviously Hammurabi was a man of war as well as a man of peace. To say that one makes wars as a way of making peace can sound like a common justification for wars of aggression. Hammurabi says his wars will end war—as, 3,700 years later, much of the world fought a "war to end all wars." (We call it World War I, and it did not work either.) As several thousand years of history have demonstrated, wars seem easier to start than to end. When we remember that Hammurabi was king of most of what is now Iraq, any claim to have created a lasting peace is painful to consider.

At the same time, it is not just to see Hammurabi as someone who was mostly a conqueror. In other places, at other times, the ideal king is a warrior. Fighting and honor are the most important characteristics, and a king who could not go out and personally crack enemy heads could not have ruled. Hammurabi would not have been successful as a Viking leader, for instance. He had other ideals. Still, he was a king of his time, and they were not peaceful times. Babylon could not have survived if Hammurabi had not fought.

So how can we judge Hammurabi and his achievements? What did he accomplish?

Certainly the role of king—the ideal king of the royal hymns—included the ability to make war. A hymn of praise for Hammurabi says, "I make people of one mind . . . I am the fear-inspiring, who, when lifting his fierce eyes, gives the disobedient the death sentence. . . ." In this hymn, the role of the fierce warrior, a "young lion, who breaks necks and scepters" is united with his role as judge and punisher of wrongs. He is—by force of weapons and of just rule—someone who creates order and unity. Much of this book has been about the ideal of kingship as it evolved over thousands of years of Mesopotamian history, even as the ruling ethnic groups changed. Insofar as we can identify what Hammurabi did, how he ruled, and what the outcome of his rule was, he was a good and powerful king, and he seems to have been—as he claims—a just and merciful one. Later Assyrian kings, in the 900s and 800s B.C., brag in words and pictures of impaling enemies on stakes, cutting off people's hands, arms, or noses, gouging out their eyes, and burning teenaged boys and girls to death. We do not have a record of Hammurabi bragging about torturing people. War is never kind, people are mutilated and tortured, and there is no doubt that some of the victims of Hammurabi's wars would be surprised at his reputation for peace. Still, Hammurabi was proud of being a fierce king, but he did not seem to take pleasure in killing. He did not ask to be remembered as someone who mutilated people.

HAMMURABI'S SON

In 1750 B.C., the kingdom of Babylon passed to Hammurabi's son Samsuiluna. Hammurabi had died or, possibly, was too sick to rule. We have only a tantalizing fragment of a letter that his son sent to an official in Larsa. The letter said that "the king is [missing word] and so I have taken my place on the throne of my father." So Hammurabi leaves us with one more mystery about his life. Still, there is no evidence of any difficulty in the transfer of power from the old king to his son. We must assume that Hammurabi died—if not then, soon after—and was buried, as were Mesopotamian kings, in a family vault, with funeral rites. His family would have buried him in a tomb, probably within the palace, and tended it with ceremony and respect.

Blessed by the gods as king, Hammurabi was able to fulfill his responsibilities by providing necessities to his subjects and building temples to the gods. His worship of the higher powers, particularly the gods Marduk and Shamash, is often depicted in carvings *(above)*, showing Hammurabi in the classic gesture of Babylonian respect.

HOW HAMMURABI IS REMEMBERED

Hammurabi was recognized by the people of his time as unusual. Although we have no record of his having identified himself as a god—instead he credits his successes to the gods, as he should—we do know that some people considered him a god, naming their children Hammurabi-ili, which means "Hammurabi is my god," explains Marc Van De Mieroop.

Hammurabi lived in a time that did not write history and if there are legends of him, as there are for Sargon, for instance, we do not have them. So Hammurabi was remembered in two ways. One was specific: Scribes had made copies of his law collection before it was removed by the Elamites in 1158 B.C. Those laws and the prologue and epilogue continued to be copied and these copies were kept in all the major libraries. So what was remembered of Hammurabi after his death was not the specifics of how he carried out his battles or the history of his reign, but that same text that was excavated between 1901 and 1902. Even after people had forgotten exactly when he lived, they remembered him as a great king who spoke with authority of justice and of the unification of the land.

Although—or because—later peoples did not remember Hammurabi as a historical figure, his name was evoked as an authority on almost any subject. His name seems to have been sort of a seal of approval. A thousand years after Hammurabi's death, a king will still claim to be descended from Hammurabi, even though he was not, and was not even sure when Hammurabi had lived. These examples tell us what Hammurabi's name and kingship meant to people after his death.

THE CONTINUING RISE OF BABYLON

The most important part of Hammurabi's legacy was how he changed Mesopotamian history for the next 1,200 to 1,400 years. Some historians have said, with truth, that his empire did not long survive him. His son Samsuiluna maintained it for another ten years, but then lost control of southern Babylon. Still, the dynasty held northern Babylon for another 155 years, only then losing control of the throne.

But it was not the end of Babylon as a city. Although there were waves of invasions by different peoples, Babylon remained the most important city in the region. So it is not that Hammu-rabi created a dynasty or a Babylonia that survived unchanged as a kingdom under his successors. And yet the region did not ever return to its 2,000-year history as a land of competing city-states, and invaders continued to (at least in part) adopt the customs and gods of the land.

Without summarizing another 1,500 years of history, it is still possible to talk about how Babylon's importance can be measured. It was the city invaders most wanted to rule. It was the city that grew larger and more elaborate as older cities like Ur disappeared. Although at times another city would gain in power, such as the city of Nimrud, in the north, in the 800s B.C., power always returned to Babylon. It was, in the words of the King Lists, "the seat of kingship." When Alexander the Great conquered it in 331 B.C., he began to restore the temple and the great ziggurat. He wanted to make the city of Babylon the capital of his empire, the capital of the world. Instead he died there, in 323 B.C. The Greek culture spread. Only then did the knowledge of cuneiform die out, not to be rediscovered until the middle of the nineteenth century, when scholars were again able to read some inscriptions about a great king named Hammurabi.

Another way to identify Babylon's continuing importance is through the rising importance of its patron god, Marduk. Originally Marduk was a minor god, as Babylon was a minor city. The important gods, the national gods of Sumer, were patrons of the original important Sumerian cities. As Babylon rose in power, Marduk did too, and this rise in power continued after Hammu-rabi's death. Marduk was understood as having more and more powers that had once belonged to other gods, although the other gods were still worshipped. In the "Epic of Creation," our earliest copy of which is from about 1200 B.C., a different version of creation is told than the one that the Sumerians and Akkadians had known. In this story, the world is created through Marduk's victory over the goddess Tiamut. The grateful gods bestow upon him 50 names and functions, all of them taken from other gods.

Even invaders respected Marduk's power. When the Elamites wanted to threaten Babylon's power, they stole the statue of Marduk from his main temple. In 539 B.C., the story goes, invaders held off invading Marduk's temple because ceremonies were going on and the priests gave the city to the invading king. Hammurabi's god was still the god of his city.

Hammurabi's Babylon would be the seat of power in the entire region for well over 1,000 years. His laws influenced future laws of the region and then of much of the Western world. Historians should never go back in time and put words in someone's mouth, especially when we have as little evidence as we do for Hammurabi. But surely the man who had his scribes and stone cutters put up that stela would be pleased that we still know it, that scholars have learned again to read it, and that nearly 4,000 years after his death, Hammurabi is still remembered as the King of Justice.

CHRONOLOGY

◆ ◆ ◆

A note about dates: About 100 years after Hammurabi's death, astronomers recorded the appearance and disappearance of the planet Venus for many years. The pattern they recorded could describe three different time periods, giving us three possible sets of dates for Hammurabi. The most commonly used one is the one in the middle, not the earliest or latest dates, and that is the one this book uses. In Hammurabi's time, the calendar began in April.

ca 2296–2240 B.C. Sargon, ruler of Akkad (Agade) unifies Mesopotamia.

1894 B.C. The beginning of the dynasty of Amorite kings in Babylonia that will produce Hammurabi.

1792 B.C. Hammurabi inherits the throne of Babylon from his father.

1791 B.C. In Hammurabi's first year as king he "forgives debts."

1776 B.C. King Shamshi-Adad, who controls Upper Mesopotamia, dies and his kingdom begins to fragment.

1775 B.C. The city-state of Mari regains independence (after being ruled by Eshnunna) under King Zimri-Lim.

1764 B.C. Hammurabi defeats Elam; his daughter is married to the new king, Silli-Sin, of Eshnunna.

1763 B.C.   Hammurabi conquers the kingdom of Larsa and its king, Rim-Sin.

1762 B.C.   Hammurbi takes over Larsa and surrounding region, renames it Yamutbal, its old name; sacks Eshnunna.

1761 B.C.   Hammurabi conquers Mari.

1759 B.C.   Hammurabi sacks Mari, destroying the city.

1756 B.C.   Hammurabi destroys Eshnunna by flooding it.

1755 B.C.   First possible date for Hammurabi's law collection monument, as it is only at this time that he controls all the regions he names in its prologue.

1750 B.C.   The last year of Hammurabi's reign; the kingdom passes to his eldest son, Samsuiluna.

1749 B.C.   Hammurabi's son's first year as king.

BIBLIOGRAPHY

◆ ◆ ◆

Bottéro, Jean. *Mesopotamia: Writing, Reasoning, and the Gods.* Chicago: The University of Chicago Press, 1992.

Kramer, Samuel Noah. *History Begins at Sumer.* Garden City, NY: Doubleday, 1959.

———."Shulgi of Ur: A Royal Hymn and a Divine Blessing." *The Jewish Quarterly Review*, New Ser., Vol. 57, The Seventy-Fifth Anniversary Volume of the Jewish Quarterly Review. (1967): 369–380.

Kuhrt, Amélie. *The Ancient Near East*, c. 3000–330 BC. 2 vols. New York: Routledge, 1995.

Leik, Gwendolyn. *The Babylonians: An Introduction.* New York: Routledge, 2003.

Nemet-Nejat, Karen Rhea. *Daily Life in Ancient Mesopotamia.* Westport, Conn.: Greenwood Press, 1998.

Oates, Joan. *Babylon.* Revised Edition. London: Thames and Hudson, 1986.

Postgate, J.N. *Early Mesopotamia: Society and Economy at the Dawn of History.* Revised Edition. London: Routledge, 1994.

Roaf, Michael. *Cultural Atlas of Mesopotamia and the Ancient Near East.* New York: Facts On File, 1990.

Roberts, J.M. *Prehistory and the First Civilizations.* (The Illustrated History of the World, vol. 1). New York: Oxford University Press, 1999.

Roth, Martha T. *Law Collections from Mesopotamia and Asia Minor*. Second Edition. Atlanta: Scholars Press, 1997.

Roux, Georges. *Ancient Iraq*. 2nd ed. New York: Penguin, 1980.

Epic of Gilgamesh, Sanders, N.K., trans. New York: Penguin, 1972.

Schmandt-Besserat, Denise. The Envelopes That Bear the First Writing. Technology and Culture, vol. 21, No. 3 (July, 1980): 357–385.

Van De Mieroop, Marc. *King Hammurabi of Babylon*. Oxford: Blackwell Publishing, 2005.

———. *A History of the Ancient Near East, ca. 3000–323 BC*. 2nd ed. Oxford: Blackwell Publishing, 2007.

FURTHER READING

◆ ◆ ◆

Editors of Time-Life. *Mesopotamia: The Mighty Kings* (Lost Civilization series). Alexandria, Va.: Time-Life Books, 1995.

Editors of Time-Life. *Sumer: Cities of Eden* (Lost Civilization series). Alexandria, Va.: Time-Life Books, 1993.

Kramer, Samuel Noah. *History Begins at Sumer*. Garden City, N.Y.: Doubleday, 1959.

Roberts, J.M. *Prehistory and the First Civilizations*. (The Illustrated History of the World, vol 1.). New York: Oxford University Press, 1999.

Epic of Gilgamesh, Sanders, N.K., trans. New York: Penguin, 1972.

PHOTO CREDITS

◆ ◆ ◆

INDEX

◆ ◆ ◆

ABOUT THE AUTHORS

◆ ◆ ◆

JUDITH LEVIN has worked in publishing for 20 years as an editor and a freelance writer. She is the author of a number of biographies, including the Chelsea House title *Hugo Chávez* in the *Modern World Leaders* series, as well as books for children and teens on history and science. She currently resides in New York City.

ARTHUR SCHLESINGER, JR. is remembered as the leading American historian of our time. He won the Pulitzer Prize for his books *The Age of Jackson* (1945) and *A Thousand Days* (1965), which also won the National Book Award. Schlesinger was the Albert Schweitzer Professor of the Humanities at the City University of New York and was involved in several other Chelsea House projects, including the series *Revolutionary War Leaders*, *Colonial Leaders*, and *Your Government*.